First World War
and Army of Occupation
War Diary
France, Belgium and Germany

36 DIVISION
107 Infantry Brigade
Royal Irish Rifles
8th Battalion
3 October 1915 - 31 August 1917

WO95/2503/1

The Naval & Military Press Ltd
www.nmarchive.com
Published in association with The National Archives

Published by

The Naval & Military Press Ltd

Unit 10 Ridgewood Industrial Park,

Uckfield, East Sussex,

TN22 5QE England

Tel: +44 (0) 1825 749494

www.naval-military-press.com

www.nmarchive.com

This diary has been reprinted in facsimile from the original. Any imperfections are inevitably reproduced and the quality may fall short of modern type and cartographic standards.

© Crown Copyright
Images reproduced by permission of The National Archives, London, England, 2015.

Contents

Document type	Place/Title	Date From	Date To
Heading	WO95/2503/1 8 Battalion Royal Irish Rifles		
Heading	36th Division 107th Infy Bde 8th Bn Roy. Irish Rif. 1915 Oct-1917 Aug		
Heading	36th Div 8th R.I. Rifles Vol I Oct To IVth Divn Nov 4-Feb 7		
War Diary	Bramshott	03/10/1915	03/10/1915
War Diary	Boulogne	04/10/1915	04/10/1915
War Diary	Flesselles	05/10/1915	05/10/1915
War Diary	St Vast-En-Chaussee	06/10/1915	08/10/1915
War Diary	Herissart	09/10/1915	09/10/1915
War Diary	Mailly Maillet	10/10/1915	18/10/1915
War Diary	Herissart	19/10/1915	19/10/1915
War Diary	St. Vast-En-Chaussee	20/10/1915	22/10/1915
War Diary	St. Leger-Les-Domart	23/10/1915	25/10/1915
Heading	10th Inf. Bde. 4th Div. Battn. Transferred From 107th Inf. Bde. 4th Div. 4.11.15 8th Battn. The Royal Irish Rifles. November (26.10.15-30.11.15) 1915		
War Diary	St. Leger-Les-Domart	26/10/1915	03/11/1915
War Diary	Puchevillers	04/11/1915	04/11/1915
War Diary	Mailly-Maillet	05/11/1915	07/11/1915
War Diary	Acheux	08/11/1915	11/11/1915
War Diary	St. Leger-Les-Domart	26/10/1915	03/11/1915
War Diary	Puchevillers	04/11/1915	04/11/1915
War Diary	Mailly-Maillet	05/11/1915	07/11/1915
War Diary	Acheux	08/11/1915	30/11/1915
Heading	107th Inf Bde. 4th Division. This Battn Was Transferred to 10th Bde 4.11.1915 8th Battn Royal Irish Rifles November 1915		
Heading	10th Inf. Bde. 4th Div. 8th Battn. The Royal Irish Rifles. December 1915		
War Diary	Trenches	01/12/1915	01/12/1915
War Diary	Auchonvillers	02/12/1915	31/12/1915
Heading	8th R. Irish Rifles Vol 2 Jan '16		
Miscellaneous	8th Irish Rifles Vol 4		
War Diary	On Service	01/01/1916	31/01/1916
Miscellaneous	Operation Orders By Lt-Colonel R.T. Pelly, D.S.O. Commanding 8th Bn Royal Irish Rifles	16/01/1916	16/01/1916
War Diary		01/02/1916	04/02/1916
War Diary	Mailly-Maillet	05/02/1916	16/02/1916
War Diary	Trenches	17/02/1916	20/02/1916
War Diary	Forceville	21/02/1916	23/02/1916
War Diary	Trenches And Mailly	24/02/1916	29/02/1916
War Diary	On Service	01/03/1916	04/03/1916
War Diary	Mailly-Maillet	05/03/1916	07/03/1916
War Diary	Trenches	08/03/1916	21/03/1916
War Diary	Mailly Maillet	22/03/1916	27/03/1916
War Diary	Trenches	28/03/1916	29/03/1916
War Diary	Mailly-Maillet	30/03/1916	30/03/1916
War Diary	Puchevillers	31/03/1916	30/04/1916
War Diary	Lealvillers	01/05/1916	07/05/1916

War Diary	Martinsart	08/05/1916	31/05/1916
Map	Trenches Left Brigade		
Heading	107th Brigade. 36th Division. 1/8th Battalion Royal Irish Rifles. June 1916		
War Diary	On Service	01/06/1916	30/06/1916
Heading	107th Brigade. 36th Division. 1/8th Battalion Royal Irish Rifles. July 1916		
War Diary		01/07/1916	31/07/1916
War Diary	In The Trenches	01/08/1916	08/08/1916
War Diary	In Billets	09/08/1916	16/08/1916
War Diary	In The Trenches	17/08/1916	24/08/1916
War Diary	In Billets	25/08/1916	31/08/1916
War Diary		01/09/1916	30/11/1916
War Diary	In The Trenches	01/12/1916	04/12/1916
War Diary	Billets	04/12/1916	09/12/1916
War Diary	In Billets	10/12/1916	10/12/1916
War Diary	In The Trenches	11/12/1916	16/12/1916
War Diary	In Billets	17/12/1916	22/12/1916
War Diary	In Trenches	23/12/1916	28/12/1916
War Diary	In Billets	29/12/1916	31/12/1916
Map			
Miscellaneous	System For Putting Out Wire Trestles		
Miscellaneous	Operation Orders By Lt. Col. R.I. Pelles, D.S.O. Comdg 8th Bn R. J. Rifles	16/01/1916	16/01/1916
War Diary		01/01/1917	31/01/1917
War Diary	On Service	01/02/1917	31/03/1917
Miscellaneous	8th Bn Royal Irish Rifles	24/03/1917	24/03/1917
War Diary	On Service	01/04/1917	17/04/1917
War Diary	2nd Army Training Area	18/04/1917	18/04/1917
War Diary	Zoudausques	19/04/1917	19/04/1917
War Diary	2nd Army Training Area	20/04/1917	20/04/1917
War Diary	Zoudausques	21/04/1917	30/04/1917
War Diary	On Service	01/05/1917	31/05/1917
War Diary	Berthen	01/06/1917	06/06/1917
War Diary	From To No 3 Area Dranoutre	06/06/1917	06/06/1917
War Diary	To Assembly Trenches	06/06/1917	06/06/1917
War Diary	Blue Line	07/06/1917	07/06/1917
War Diary	Fort Victoria	08/06/1917	09/06/1917
War Diary	No 3 Area	10/06/1917	13/06/1917
War Diary	No 13 Area	14/06/1917	17/06/1917
War Diary	Fort Victoria	18/06/1917	19/06/1917
War Diary	Trenches	20/06/1917	30/06/1917
Operation(al) Order(s)	Operation Orders No 105 5th June 1917	05/06/1917	05/06/1917
Miscellaneous	Secret Order 6th June 1917	06/06/1917	06/06/1917
Miscellaneous	Contact Patrols Appendix "H"		
Miscellaneous	Code Letters For Liaison Between Infantry & Aircraft		
Miscellaneous	Summary Of Offensive Operations On 7th June, 1917 By 8th Battalion Royal Irish Rifles		
Miscellaneous	Special Order By Major-General O.S.W. Nugent, C.B., D.S.O. Commanding 36th (Ulster) Division	06/07/1917	06/07/1917
War Diary	On Service	01/07/1917	31/08/1917

WO 95/2503/1

8 Battalion Royal Irish Rifles

36TH DIVISION
107TH INFY BDE

8TH BN ROY. IRISH RIF.

~~OCT 1915 &~~
~~FEB 1916-JAN 1918~~

1915 OCT — 1917 AUG

8 BN amalgamated with 9 BN
SEP 1917

8th R. i. Rifles
Vol: I

121 Oct.
———
78924   To IV Divn
Nov. 4 - Feb 7

36 h/fsi

8th (Service) Batt. The Royal IRISH RIFLES

WAR DIARY
or
INTELLIGENCE SUMMARY.
(Erase heading not required.)

Army Form C. 2118.

Remarks column: R.I. Batt. 8. R.I. Rif. 8th (Service) Batt. R.I. Rifles

Place	Date	Hour	Summary of Events and Information
Bramshott	3.10.15		The Battn. left BRAMSHOTT and proceeded to FOLKESTONE where they embarked & after an uneventful passage arrived at BOULOGNE at about midnight. The Battn. came across in two parties with about 1 hours interval.
Boulogne	4.10.15		The Battn. went into a rest camp at OSTREHOVE. The Battn. entrained at 7 p.m. & proceeded to FLESSELLES.
Flesselles	5.10.15		At 2 a.m. the Battn. detrained and proceeded to ST VAST-EN-CHAUSSEE where they went into billets.
St Vast-en-Chaussée	6.10.15		The Battn. remained in billets.
" "	7.10.15		The Battn. remained in billets.
" "	8.10.15		The 107th Bde. were inspected by the 3rd Army Commdt. at VIGNACOURT
Hérissart	9.10.15		The Battn. proceeded to HERISSART where they went into billets
Mailly-Maillet	10.10.15		The Battn. proceeded to MAILLY-MAILLET.
	11.10.15		At 5 p.m. the Battn. went into the trenches. One coy. being attached for instruction to each of the following regiments. MONMOUTHS. - LANC. FUSRS. - KING'S OWN. - ESSEX. There were no casualties.

Army Form C. 2118.

8th R I Rifles

WAR DIARY
or
INTELLIGENCE SUMMARY
(Erase heading not required.)

Instructions regarding War Diaries and Intelligence Summaries are contained in F. S. Regs., Part II. and the Staff Manual respectively. Title pages will be prepared in manuscript.

Place	Date	Hour	Summary of Events and Information	Remarks and references to Appendices
MAILLY-MAILLET	12.10.15		Battn. still in trenches and attached to other units for instruction. No casualties.	R T Bell Lt-Col Comdg 8. R. I. Rifles
MAILLY-MAILLET	13.10.15		Battn. was taken over by 10th Brigade and in the trenches were attached to the Dublins, Royal Irish Fusiliers, Warwicks, and Seaforths who relieved the other battalions in the evening. There were no casualties. MAJOR BURNAND of the Munsters joined the Battn. and took over the duties of 2nd in Command.	
MAILLY-MAILLET	14.10.15		Battn. still in the trenches. No casualties.	
MAILLY-MAILLET	15.10.15		Battn. still in the trenches. 2nd Lt R. McC. PETTIGREW of "C" Coy. received bullet wound in cheek, and admitted to hospital same day. He was sent to England 22/10/15.	
MAILLY-MAILLET	16.10.15		Battn. still in the trenches. Rfn. A. EDGAR no 8/160 "D" Coy reported missing.	
MAILLY-MAILLET	17.10.15		Battn. in trenches till evening, when they returned to billets in MAILLY-MAILLET. Rfn H.H. REYNOLDS no 8/1973 "D" Coy sent to hospital with slight shrapnel wound. "A" Coy spent night in Auchonvillers.	
MAILLY-MAILLET	18.10.15		Battn. left MAILLY-MAILLET and marched to HERISSART, where they went into billets.	
HERISSART	19.10.15		Battn. left HERISSART and marched to St. VAST-EN-CHAUSSEE, where they went into billets.	
St.VAST-EN-CHAUSSEE	20.10.15		Battn. remained in billets. Genl. Withycombe assumes Command of Bde.	
"	21.10.15		Battn. remained in billets. Divisional Field day under Genl. Nugent Comdg.	
"	22.10.15		Battn. left St VAST-EN-CHAUSSEE and marched to St LEGER-LES-DOMART, where they went into billets.	
St LEGER-LES-DOMART	23.10.15		Battn. remained in billets.	
"	24.10.15		Battn. remained in billets.	
"	25.10.15		Battn. marched to VERT-GALAND on PARIS to AMIENS road, and lined route for the KING.	

10th Inf.Bde.
4th Div.

Battn. transferred
from 107th Inf.Bde.
4th Div. 4.11.15.

8th BATTN. THE ROYAL IRISH RIFLES.

N O V E M B E R

(26.10.15 - 30.11.15)

1 9 1 5

Army Form C. 2118

WAR DIARY
or
INTELLIGENCE SUMMARY
(Erase heading not required.)

8th R.Irish Rifles

Bn transferred to 10th Bde on 4th November 1915

Place	Date	Hour	Summary of Events and Information	Remarks and references to Appendices
ST.LEGER-LES-DOMART	26.10.15. 27th		Battalion remained in billets.	
	28th		" " " "	
	29th		" " " "	
	30th		" " " "	
	31st		" " " "	
	1.11.15.		" " " "	
	2nd		" " " "	
	3rd		Battalion left ST.LEGER-LES-DOMART and marched to PUCHEVILLERS, where they went into billets.	
PUCHEVILLERS	4th		Battalion left PUCHEVILLERS, and "C" & "D" Coy with H.Q. marched to MAILLY-MAILLET, "B" Coy to COLINCAMPS, and "A" Coy to AUCHONVILLERS, where they went into billets. Battalion attached to 10th Brigade. General HULL commanding.	
MAILLY-MAILLET	5th		Companies occupied their respective billets as noted on 4.11.15.	
"	6th		" " " " " " " " "	
"	7th		Companies left their respective billets and marched in the evening to ACHEUX, where they went into billets.	
ACHEUX	8th		Battalion remained in billets	
"	9th		" " " "	
"	10th		" " " "	
"	11th		" " " "	

R.T.Pelly,
Lt.Colonel,
Comdg. 8th R.I.Rifles.

Army Form C. 2118.

WAR DIARY
or
INTELLIGENCE SUMMARY.
(Erase heading not required.)

10th Bde
Oct 26th – Nov 30
Transferred Nov 4th to IVth Divn

8 R.D. Rif
R.T. Betty Lt-Col
Comdg 8. R.D Rifles

Place	Date	Hour	Summary of Events and Information	Remarks and references to Appendices
St. LEGER-LES-DOMART	26.10.15		Battn remained in billets.	
"	27.10.15		" " " "	
"	28.10.15		" " " "	
"	29.10.15		" " " "	
"	30.10.15		" " " "	
"	31.10.15		" " " "	
"	1.11.15		" " " "	
"	2.11.15		" " " "	
"	3.11.15		Battn left St. LEGER-LES-DOMART, and marched to PUCHEVILLERS, where they went into billets.	
PUCHEVILLERS	4.11.15		Battn left PUCHEVILLERS, "C" and "D" Coy with H.Q marched to MAILLY-MAILLET, "B" Coy to COLINCAMPS, and "A" Coy to AUCHONVILLERS, where they went into billets. Battn attached to 10th Brigade. General HULL commanding.	
MAILLY-MAILLET	5.11.15		COMPANIES occupied their respective billets as noted on 4.11.15.	
"	6.11.15		" " " "	
"	7.11.15		Companies left their respective billets and marched in the evening to ACHEUX, where they went into billets.	
ACHEUX	8.11.15		Battn remained in billets	
"	9.11.15		" " " "	
"	10.11.15		" " " "	
"	11.11.15		" " " "	

WAR DIARY
or
INTELLIGENCE SUMMARY.

Army Form C. 2118.

Place	Date	Hour	Summary of Events and Information	Remarks and references to Appendices
Acheux	12/11/15		Remained in Billets	
	13		" " "	
	14		Left for trenches "A" Coy with 7th Argylls "B" Coy 2nd Dubs "C" Coy Warwicks D Coy Bedforths	
	15		In Trenches.	No 8/12619 Rfm S. Beattie Killed. No 8/15223 . J. McClurg Wounded
	16		— " — No 8/13158 Rfm N. McIntosh, wounded	
	17		— " — No 8/13213 " E. McAvoy, wounded.	
	18		Relieved, A Coy by 9th R. Ir. Fus & marched to Colincamps. No 8/13448 Rfm T. Robinson Wounded	R. I. Rifle
	19		Relieved, B. C & D to Colincamps No 8/13246 Rfm J. C. Shillington reported missing	
	20		Bn. marched to Mailly Maillet, into Billets No 8/296 Rfm J. Kerr Wounded at Duty	Lieut J. E. Shillington reported missing Rfm A. Magee. Died of Wounds
	21		In Billets	
	22		— " —	
	23		— " — Lieut W. L. Campbell 2nd R. Ir. Regt joined & took over duties of Adjutant	
	24		— " — Lieut A. M. Moore. Wounded.	
	25		— " — Lecture on Gas.	
	26		To Trenches, occupied my 1st Sector, 2nd R. Ir. Regt 2nd Royal Dubs on left.	
	27		In Trenches,	
	28		— " — Lt L. Hunter, Missing, also No 8/3423 Rfm W. Dilworth	J. Agnew Missing
	29		— " — " 8/3115 " R. Brown	
	30		— " — " 8/3695	

107th Inf Bde.
4th Division.
This Battn was Transfered
to 10th Bde 4. 11. 1915

8th Batnn ROYAL IRISH RIFLES

N O V E M B E R   1 9 1 5

10th Inf.Bde.
4th Div.

8th BATTN. THE ROYAL IRISH RIFLES.

D E C E M B E R

1 9 1 5

8th R. I. Rifles

Army Form C. 2118.

WAR DIARY
or
INTELLIGENCE SUMMARY.
(Erase heading not required.)

Margin notes: Bondy 8th R.I. Rifles / R.T.P.M. Lt-Col.

Place	Date	Hour	Summary of Events and Information	Remarks and references to Appendices
TRENCHES Auchonvillers	1/12/15		In Trenches — Capt. J.W. Laidley 2nd Royal Scots rejoins his Regt.	
	2		Relieved by 9th R. Ir. Rifles & went into Billets at FORCEVILLE	
	3		In Billets	
	4		" — Bn were lectured by Argylls in Lambton Cup.	
	5		"	
	6		"	
	7		"	
	8		"	
	9		To Trenches occupied right sector. (2nd R. Ir. Regt on our right 2nd Dubs left)	
	10		In Trenches No 8/12405 Rfm D. Quinn slightly wounded (at Duty)	
	11		" — 2nd Lieut J. Murphy joined & was posted to "B" Coy.	
	12		" No 8/13810 Rfm W. Walker, wounded 11-12-15.	
	13		Relieved by 9th R. Ir. Rifles, marched to Billets at Vattenes.	
	14		In Billets (Lecture on Cromwell's campaigns in Flanders, at Acheux) (Prof Fletcher)	
	15		— (Draft of 62 men joined Bn.)	
	16		—	
	17		"A" Coy Collincamps, "B" Coy Auchonvillers, "C" Coy Elles Square, "D" Coy Mailloy (Bde Reserve)	
	18		" — 1 Platoon "A" Coy at "La Signy" 2nd Lieut Curtin joined. No 9/97 Rfn J. Townley wounded No 8/12795 — A. Gillespie	

WAR DIARY
or
INTELLIGENCE SUMMARY.
(Erase heading not required.)

Army Form C. 2118.

Instructions regarding War Diaries and Intelligence Summaries are contained in F.S. Regs., Part II. and the Staff Manual respectively. Title pages will be prepared in manuscript.

Place	Date	Hour	Summary of Events and Information	Remarks and references to Appendices
Noulette	19.12.15		Coys as for 18th. No 12/592 Rfn J. Loursley died of wounds & was buried at Nœux les Mines. No 100 was evacuated.	
	20.12.15		as for 19th	
	21.12.15		as for 20	
	22.12.15		To Trenches. occupied Right sector in relief of 7th R.D.F. (2nd R.I Rgt) 11th Bn. 8/322 Rfn S. Moorhead 9th R.I Rifles left of Bn.)	
	23.12.15		In Trenches. Weather very bad 9/327 J. McKinstry } wounded	
			,, Retaliated there were no casualties on our side. our Artillery carried out a bombardment German	
	24.12.15		In Trenches. Weather extremely bad. flooded trenches everywhere.	
	25.12.15		,, Xmas day. Lewis Gun under 2nd Lt. Adermithy caught a small party of Germans emerging from a sap – thought to be a working party – Two of the party are seen to fall. No greetings were exchanged. opened fire at every opportunity Relieved by 1 Bn. The Rgnd Irish Fusiliers at 7.45 P.M.	
	26.12.15		In Billets. Vermelles Had a Christmas free issue of beer.	
	27.12.15		,, Bn to follow	
	28.12.15		,, ,, Bn to follow	
	29.12.15		Relieved 1st Reg:al Irish Fusiliers in right sector at 7.P.M.	
	30.12.15		In Trenches. Quiet day. Day matter Lt-Col Pelly took over command of Batt from Lt Col R.J. Church D.S.O. 2nd Royal Irish Reg. on our right. 9th R.I. Rifles on our left.	
	31.12.15		Quiet day Heavy firing along German line late at night. No result.	

8th R. Irish Rifles
Vol: 2

Jan 716

8th Irish Rifles
Vol 4

WAR DIARY

INTELLIGENCE SUMMARY

Army Form C. 2118.

(Erase heading not required.)

Place	Date	Hour	Summary of Events and Information	Remarks and references to Appendices
On Service.	1/1/16		Bn in occupation of trenches of right section E of Auchonvillers, 9th R.I. Rifles on left, 2nd R.I. Regt on right.	
	2/1/16		Bn in same position. Quiet day. 5/3098 Cpl W. McD. slightly wounded by shrapnel.	
	3/1/16		Bn in same position. Nothing unusual to report.	
	4/1/16		Bn relieved by 10th R.I. Rifles. Proceeded to billets in Varennes. Draft of 37 arrived.	
	5/1/16		Bn in billets in Varennes.	
	6/1/16		" " " " Supplied working parties on Corps line.	
	7/1/16		" " " " 2nd Lt. A. B. Cooke joined the Bn. Supplied working parties on front line.	
	8/1/16		Left for trenches and took over right sector from 10th R.I. Rifles.	
			In Trenches. 5/12249 Rfm E. Brennan wounded. 2nd Lt. W. McDermott. 5/12357 Cpl H. Murphy. 17/837 Rfm G.P. Connor } killed. 2nd Lt. W. McDermott, Cpl Murphy & Rfm Connor buried at Auchonvillers.	
	9/1/16		" by Rev Mitchell.	
	10/1/16		In Trenches. Nothing unusual.	
	11/1/16		Relieved by 10th R.I. Rifles and returned to billets Mailly-Maillet.	
	12/1/16		Billets. Mailly-Maillet.	
	13/1/16		" " "	
	14/1/16		" " "	
	15/1/16		To Trenches and took over from 10th R.I. Rifles.	
	16/1/16		Trenches. Made preparations to straighten line by advancing 100 yds on a front of 500-600 yds. 5/12357 Rfm W. Marshall, 17/785 Rfm J. Gordon were slightly	

Army Form C. 2118.

WAR DIARY
or
INTELLIGENCE SUMMARY.
(Erase heading not required.)

Instructions regarding War Diaries and Intelligence Summaries are contained in F. S. Regs., Part II. and the Staff Manual respectively. Title pages will be prepared in manuscript.

Place	Date	Hour	Summary of Events and Information	Remarks and references to Appendices
On Service	16/1/6. 17/1/6.		wounded during this operation.	
			As francke. The day passed quietly. Carrying parties took material up to front trench during morning for use in constructing new trench.	
		5.15 p.m.	Covering parties went out under Lt. Murphy. Reported all clear at 5.45 p.m.	
		5.45 p.m.	Wiring parties under Lieuts. P. Murray & C.C. Curtin went out and commenced work.	
		6 p.m.	Three working parties of the 10th C. S. Rifles filed on to their tasks and started digging.	
		11 p.m.	Covering parties relieved by similar parties under 2t. Briggs-ok.	
		11.30 p.m.	Digging parties filed out.	
		11.35 p.m.	Enemy opened Heavy shell and machine gun fire on their task.	
		11.40 p.m.	Our artillery replied.	
		11.45 p.m.	All quiet again. 2nd relief of digging parties filed on to their task & commenced work.	
	18.1.16	2 a.m.	Wiring parties withdrew, having completed a double row of high entanglements along the whole of the new task (500 yds)	
		2.30 a.m.	Sentries posted in the new trench.	
		3 a.m.	Covering parties withdrawn.	
		4 a.m.	Digging parties ceased work and new trench manned by garrison of old.	
		4.30 a.m.	Digging parties marched home by their respective routes.	
			The operation was a complete success and was carried out with the loss of only two men wounded.	
			Everything was carried out exactly as laid down in the operation orders and there was no hitch of any kind.	
			The Br. was highly complimented on the work by the Brigadier, Brig.-Genl. D. H. Withycombe, C. of C. G. and by the Divisional Commander, Major General Hon. W. Lambton.	
			A copy of operation orders is attached.	

Army Form C. 2118.

WAR DIARY
INTELLIGENCE SUMMARY.
(Erase heading not required.)

Instructions regarding War Diaries and Intelligence Summaries are contained in F. S. Regs., Part II. and the Staff Manual respectively. Title pages will be prepared in manuscript.

Place	Date	Hour	Summary of Events and Information	Remarks and references to Appendices
On Service.	18.1.16.	4.30 a.m.	No 5/13400 Sgt W. H. Purdy & 17/606 Pte D. McKittrick were slightly wounded. The remainder of the day passed in comparative calm.	
		6 p.m.	Deepening and improving line of new trench and wiring continued.	
	19.1.16		No 5/11524 Pte W. Bain, 5/3162 Pte D. Stothers & 14012 Pte J. Kennedy were wounded. Pte Old or Pte Lance Sgt (Ruston [illegible]) heavily shelled between 7 & 8.15 a.m. there were no casualties. Relieved at 8 p.m. by 10th R.S. Coys and returned to Billets in Vavrenne.	
	20.1.16		In Billets	
	21.1.16.		" "	
	22.1.16		The Corps Commander inspected the last two drafts. Board for testing men for making munitions visited the Bn and found it capable men who will be called for in due course.	
	23.1.16.		In Billets. Relieved 10th Bn in trenches between 6 & 8 p.m.	
	24.1.16.		In Trenches. Divisional Commander inspected new line of trenches	
	25.1.16		" "	Normal
	26.1.16		" "	
	27		" "	Relieved by 10" Bn. 8.30 p.m. returned to Billets mostly hotel
	28			
	29		In Billets hotels	
	30			
	31.1.16		To Trenches Relieved 10" Bn.	

R.T. Pelly Lt Colonel.
Comm'dg 6th Bn. Royal Irish Rifles
Oulaige
1-2-16

SECRET.

Operation Orders
by
Lt-Colonel R.T.Pelly, D.S.O.
Commanding 8th Bn Royal Irish Rifles.

16th January 1916.

1. To-morrow night(17th-18th)the right portion of our line from saps 1 to 4 inclusive will be advanced,a new trench being dug linking up these four sap heads. The cutting line will be taped out in readiness to-night and Officers in charge of working parties shown the ground.

2. COVERING PARTY. - A covering party consisting of 4 squads of 1 N.C.O. and 6 men each,the whole under the command of Lt Murphy will work out to beyond the crest of HAWTHORN RIDGE,one squad starting out from each sap, so as to be in position at 6.30 p.m.
   A report will be sent to No 3 sap when the covering party is in position.
   This party will relieved by a similar party under Lt Maharty at 11.30 p.m.

3. WIRING PARTIES. - No 1 wiring party(Sgt Stewart and 12 men)will complete and strengthen the existing wires between saps 1 and 2.
   No 2 wiring party(Cpl Johnson and 12 men) will complete and strengthen the existing wire between saps 2 and 3. These two parties will be under Lt P.Murray.
   No 3 wiring party(Lt Curtin,Sgt Hyde and 20 men) will construct an entanglement between saps 3 and 4.
   Material will be dumped for these parties as follows:-
   For No 1 party at the head of No 1 sap.
       No 2 " " " " No 2 "
       No 3 " " " " No 4 "
   Gaps 1 yard wide will be left in the entanglement immediately at the South Side of each sap head.
   Wiring parties will commence work at 6 p.m.

DIGGING PARTIES.

1st Relief.
3 Digging parties will be furnished by the 10th Bn R.I.Rifles.
No 1(2 Officers and 75 men) will march from AUCHONVILLERS by the light railway to railhead in 2nd Avenue, thence by a track across country marked with a trail of chloride of lime to the front trench and so via No 2 sap to their task which will be between No 1 and 2 saps extending on it to the right. A guide will meet them at the 2nd Avenue railhead.
No 2 (2 Officers and 75 men)will march via 2nd Avenue to No 3 sap and extend to the right on their task which will be from No 3 sap to No 2.
No 3 (2 Officers and 125 men)will march via OLD BEAUMONT ROAD to No 4 sap and extend to the right on their task which will be from No 4 sap to No 3.
The 1st relief will work from 6 p.m. to 12 m.n.
At 12 m.n. each man of this relief will lay his tools down on the part of his task and the parties will file away by their respective saps, turning to the right (North)into the fire trench on leaving the sap. When the last man is clear of the sap these parties will get on the firestep, leaving the trench clear until the next relief have filed down the saps to their tasks

2nd Relief will be of equal strength to the 1st Relief.
The 3 parties will proceed by the routes detailed for the 1st relief and will be at their respective entrances to the fire trench at 12 m.n. They will not enter the fire trench until receiving word that the 1st relief is clear and on the firestep.
This relief will continue work until ordered to leave by O.C.8th Bn R.I.Rifles,when they will depart by the routes they came taking their tools with them.

Operation Orders (Contd)

4. **CASUALTIES.**

Any casualties will be evacuated by the chloride of lime path or OLD BEAUMONT ROAD to AUCHONVILLERS.

A stretcher party will be in the fire trench near the mouth of each sap.

5. **BATTN HD QRS.**

Battn Hd Qrs will be established at the Hd Qrs of the Right Coy in 2nd Avenue, where all reports will be sent.

6. **COMMUNICATION.**

Telephone communication will be established between Bn Hd Qrs (vide 5) and each sap head.

7. **DRESS.**

Wiring and digging parties will wear one bandolier of ammunition and carry their rifles which will be loaded with 5 rounds before starting No equipment or bayonets will be worn by these parties.

Sgd. W.L.Campbell, Lieut & Adjt
6th Bn R.I.Rifles.

Army Form C. 2118.

WAR DIARY
or
INTELLIGENCE SUMMARY.

(Erase heading not required.)

8th (Ser.) Bn. ROYAL IRISH RIFLES

Instructions regarding War Diaries and Intelligence Summaries are contained in F. S. Regs., Part II. and the Staff Manual respectively. Title pages will be prepared in manuscript.

Place	Date	Hour	Summary of Events and Information	Remarks and references to Appendices.
	1/2/16		In Trenches	
	2/2/16		" "	Normal. No casualties
	3		" "	
	4		" "	Relieved by 10th B. 8.5 PM and moved back to Billets Mailly
Mailly-Maillet	5		In billets. Supplied working parties to extent of two Offs & 60 OR.
	6			109th Brigade transferred to 36th Division
				4th Division relieved by 36th Division. For the present 8th & 10th B"s occupy same sector.
				The Battalion when at rest will be quartered at Mailly.
	7/2/16		2nd Bn Royal Irish Regiment (18th Foot) relieved by 11th Bn R.I. Rifles, marched out our type band was placed at their disposal and was accepted with many thanks. The Band headed the Royal Irish Regt. and played them to VARENNES. The music was much appreciated by Officers and men. Col Dugan who commanded the 2nd R I Regt. again sent thanks for kindness in allowing the band to accompany them.
			Battn inspected by Gen. Nugent comdg 36th Div. who during the course of his short address, welcomed the Battn back to Div. and gave high words of praise in reference to our good work whilst with the 4th Div.	
	8/2/16		Relieved 10 & 13th in trenches occupying same sector, 11th Bn R.I.R. on our right and the 9th R.I.R. on our left.
			The B"s was distributed as follows:—
			"A" Coy = Right of Sector
			"B" " = Left " "
			"C" " = 3 Platoons "POMPADOUR" } Supports
			1 " "CARDIFF STREET" }
			" BEAUMONT ROAD
			"D" = Defence Coy AUCHONVILLERS

WAR DIARY or INTELLIGENCE SUMMARY

Army Form C. 2118.

8th (Ser.) Bn. ROYAL IRISH RIFLES

(Erase heading not required.)

Instructions regarding War Diaries and Intelligence Summaries are contained in F. S. Regs., Part II. and the Staff Manual respectively. Title pages will be prepared in manuscript.

Place	Date	Hour	Summary of Events and Information	Remarks and references to Appendices
	9/2/16		In Trenches 8/12252 Sgt R. Dunn wounded	
	10/2/16		" 8/12 530 Sgt J. Allen wounded, 17/13144 Rfn H. McWilliams killed in action	
	11/2/16		" burned same day at Authuille	
	12/2/16	8.50 PM	" 8/32.09 Rfn A. Gordon wounded	
			Relieved by 10th & 13th R.I. Rifles and returned to billets at Mailly.	
Mailly-Maillet	13-2-16		In Billets, working parties to extent of 400 Officers and other ranks	
	14-2-16		"	
	15-2-16		"	
	16-2-16		To Trenches. Major Peacock 3 Officers 108 Other Ranks 9th Innis. Fus.	
			attached to Battalion for instruction. 3 --- 54 --- 14th R.I.R. (Y.C.V.)	
Trenches	17-2-16		In Trenches 9th B" on our Left, 11th Innis. Fus on our Right.	
	18-2-16		"	
	19-2-16		" Trench on our left. Glove District was heavily bombarded.	
	20-2-16		" Relieved by 10th & 13th and returned to Billets at Forceville.	
			Detachments of 9th Innis Fus & 14th R.I.R. rejoined their respective units.	
Forceville	21-2-16		In Billets	
	22-2-16		" No Working parties. Had an opportunity of parades and a short Route March.	
	23-2-16		"	

R.T. Pelly
Lieut-Colonel
Comdg 8th (Ser.) Bn. ROYAL IRISH RIFLES

Army Form C. 2118.

WAR DIARY
or
INTELLIGENCE SUMMARY.
(Erase heading not required.)

8th (Ser) Bn. ROYAL IRISH RIFLES

Instructions regarding War Diaries and Intelligence Summaries are contained in F.S. Regs., Part II. and the Staff Manual respectively. Title pages will be prepared in manuscript.

Place	Date	Hour	Summary of Events and Information	Remarks and references to Appendices
Trenches and Mailly	24-2-16		Trenches took over RIGHT SECTOR from 11th Innis Fus. The Battalion now located as follows:— "A" Coy - Right of New Sector "B" " - Left " " "C" " - Bde Reserve MAILLY "D" " - " " " "B" Hd. Qrs MAILLY	
	25-2-16		Advanced Hd Qrs for the trenches. Major N.G. Burnand Lt Reilley sick.	
	26-2-16		As for evening of 24th inst. Heavy snow-storm.	
	27-2-16		Working parties from MAILLY RESERVE to extent of 300 Officers and men	
	28-2-16		A & B Coys relieved by C & D Coys as follows:— "C" Coy - Right of Right Sector "D" " - Left " " " "A" " - Bde Reserve MAILLY. "B" " - " " " "B" Hd Qrs MAILLY.	
	29-2-16		Advanced Hd. Qrs for trenches - Lt Col. R.J. Pelly, D.S.O. Trenches very bad, caving in in places. As for evening of 28th inst.	

Army Form C. 2118.

WAR DIARY
or
INTELLIGENCE SUMMARY.
(Erase heading not required.)

Instructions regarding War Diaries and Intelligence Summaries are contained in F. S. Regs., Part II. and the Staff Manual respectively. Title pages will be prepared in manuscript.

Place	Date	Hour	Summary of Events and Information	Remarks and references to Appendices
On service	1-3-16		Normal "A" Coy relieved "C" Coy.	Col Q
	2-3-16		" "B" Coy relieved "D" Coy	Col Q
	3-3-16		"	Col Q
	4-3-16		Line taken over by 9th R.I. Fus. "A" & "B" Coys to Billets, Mailly	
Mailly-Maillet	5-3-16		In Billets	Col Q
	6-3-16		"	
	7-3-16		Took over right sector from 10th R.I.R.	
Trenches	8-3-16		In Trenches } Normal. Much snow and frost. Trenches very bad.	Midhurst. Majr Connely S.B. & A.Q 1st Rifles
	9-3-16		In Trenches }	
	10-3-16		"	
	11-3-16		Relieved by 10th R.I.R., returned to Billets at Mailly	Adm Q
	12-3-16		"	Col Q
	13-3-16		In billets	Col Q
	14-3-16		" Normal. Working Parties to extent of 200. Had opportunity of doing Battalion Drill on two occasions. Good weather.	
	15-3-16		" To Trenches in relief of 10th B. R.I. Rifles.	
	16-3-16		St. Patricks day. Very quiet. Distributed shamrock	Col Q
	17-3-16		In trenches. Normal. Weather changeable	Col Q
	18-3-16		No 8/12272 L/Cpl D. Girvan wounded. 17/10·32 Rfn S. Cassels wounded	
	19-3-16		17/10·32 " S. Cassels died of wounds	
	20-3-16		relieved by 10th R.I.R.	Col Q
	21-3-16			Col Q

Army Form C. 2118.

WAR DIARY
or
INTELLIGENCE SUMMARY.
(Erase heading not required.)

Instructions regarding War Diaries and Intelligence Summaries are contained in F. S. Regs., Part II and the Staff Manual respectively. Title pages will be prepared in manuscript.

Place	Date	Hour	Summary of Events and Information	Remarks and references to Appendices
Mailly-Maillet	22-3-16		Maj-Gen. O. S. W. Nugent D.S.O. Comdg 36th Div. inspected Regimental Transport. Many complimentary remarks were made, saying the Transport was a credit to the Battalion	
	23-3-16			
	24-3-16		In Billets. Working Parties small which allowed of Route Marching etc.	
	25-3-16			
	26-3-16		To trenches in Relief of 10th R.I.R.	
	27-3-16			
Trenches	28-3-16		In trenches	
	29-3-16		Relieved by 15th Bn West Yorks Regt (from Egypt). Left Major Burnand, Lieut Blackwood, Thornton, Crawford, & Maxwell & 16 O.Rs for purpose of instructing New Bn. (15 West Yorks) in the Trenches	
Mailly-Maillet	30-3-16	8 a.m.	A & B Coys left Mailly-Maillet for Puchevillers (12 miles march)	
		6 P.M.	Hd. Qrs & C & D Coys left Mailly-Maillet and arrived Puchevillers 10.15 P.M. Both parties marched extremely well and not a man fell out.	
Puchevillers	31-3-16		Resting. 3 Officers, 10 ofrs, 200 men working party on New Railway Line.	

8 Irish Rifles
Vol 3
xxxvi

WAR DIARY
or
INTELLIGENCE SUMMARY

Army Form C. 2118.

Place	Date	Hour	Summary of Events and Information	Remarks and references to Appendices
Picherville	1/4/16		Nothing of importance to report. The Baths furnished working parties up to 21st incl- were relieved by West Riding Reg'ts, 49th Div. Received complimentary letter from O.C. 109th Railway Coy:— "May I express my thanks to you for the good work done by your parties despite the bad weather of the past few days."	8th R.I. Rifles Lieut- Colonel Comdg 8th Bn R.I. Rifles.
	2			
	3			
	4			
	5			
	6			
	7			
	8			
	9			
	10			
	11			
	12			
	13			
	14			
	15			
	16			
	17			
	18			
	19			
	20			
	21			
	22			
	23/4/16	9 a.m.	March to Lealvillers and billeted. Entertained by 10th Bn Royal Irish Rifles on arrival.	
	24/4/16		Practised attack against dummy trenches at Blairjaye.	
	25			
	26			
	27			
	28		Practice attack.	
	29		Working parties. 6 officers, 400 O.R.	
	30		Working parties and Bayonet fighting, etc.	

Army Form C. 2118.

WAR DIARY
or
INTELLIGENCE SUMMARY.
(Erase heading not required.)

8th Irish Rifles
vol 6
XXXIII

Place	Date	Hour	Summary of Events and Information	Remarks and references to Appendices
LEALVILLERS	1-5-16		Battalion attack Practice, morning	
	2-5-16		" " " afternoon, splendid weather. Bayonet fighting and Musketry during interval	
	3-5-16		" " " morning	
	4-6-16		Brigade attack Practice. Battalion did extremely well.	
	5-5-16		Attack Pratice over 109th Brigade area.	
	6-5-16		" " " General Nugent, 36th Div. Commander present	
	7-5-16		" " "	
MARTINSART	8-5-16		Moved into Huts in Martinsart Wood. Marched near VARENNES and HEDAUVILLE. The huts were comfortable. Brig-General complimented Col Pelly on the smart turn-out of the Battalion - March discipline etc.	
	9-5-16		Working parties to extent of 10 Officers, 520 O Ranks - Informed that B" (whole Brigade) would furnish nothing but working parties during their stay in Martinsart Wood. This gave the Officers and NCO's an opportunity of instructing new area to be taken over by the Battalion.	
	10-5-16		Working Parties	
	11-5-16		" "	
	12-5-16		" "	No 17/811 L/Cpl W Cunningham, wounded on working party.
	13-5-16		" "	
	14-5-16		" "	
	15-5-16		" "	
	16-5-16		" "	
	17-5-16		" "	{16 8/12335 Cpl J McCallum wounded on working party
	18-5-16		" "	{ " 7/1372 Rfm G Ogram " " "
	19-5-16		" "	
	20-5-16		" "	

R.T. Bell
Lt Col
Comdg 8th R.Ir Rifles

WAR DIARY
or
INTELLIGENCE SUMMARY.

(Erase heading not required.)

Army Form C. 2118.

Place	Date	Hour	Summary of Events and Information	Remarks and references to Appendices
MARTINSART	21-5-16		Working Parties	
	22 "		"	
	23 "		"	
	24 "		"	
	25 "		"	
	26 "		"	
	27 "		"	
	28 "		"	
	29 "		"	
	30 "		"B" Coys. under Captain J.D. McCallum, in support to 9th R.I. Rifles, and occupied dug-outs in Thiepval Wood. 4 Lewis Guns accompanied them. "A" Coy, "C" and "D" Companies moved into Martinsart Village.	
	31 "		"B" Coys in support to 9th R.I. Rifles who occupy right sector in front of Thiepval. "A" Coys, "C" & "D" Companies, Martinsart. Inspections and refitting.	

R.T. Pelly, Lt. Col.
Comdg. 8th R.I. Royal Irish Rifles

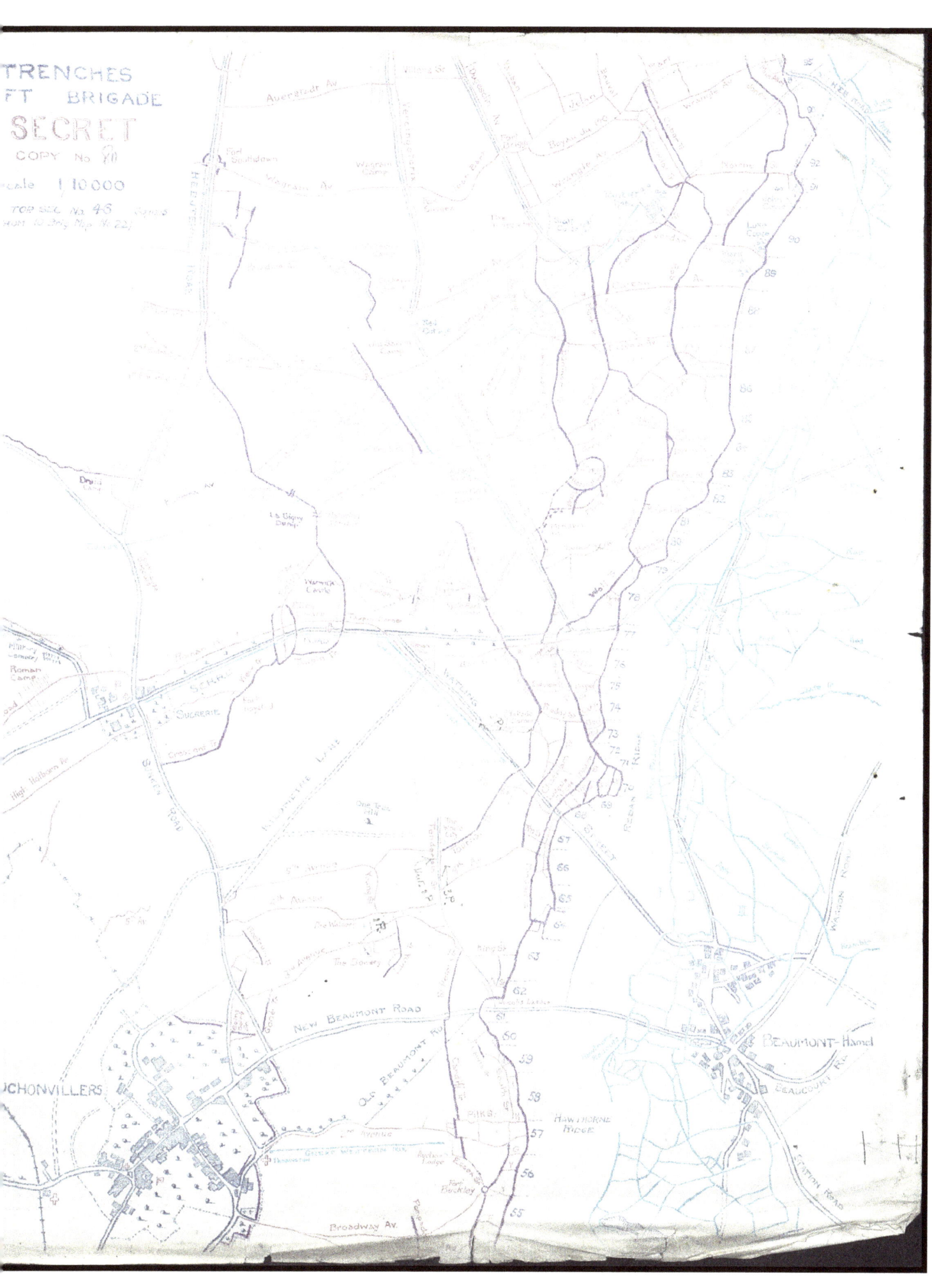

107th Brigade.
36th Division.

1/8th BATTALION

ROYAL IRISH RIFLES.

JUNE 1916:

WAR DIARY

Army Form C. 2118

10/7/16 **8. R. Ir. Rif. Vol 7**

June

Place	Date	Hour	Summary of Events and Information	Remarks and references to Appendices
On Service.	1/6/16.		"A" & "B" Coys in support to 9th R. I. Rifles who occupy right sector in front of Thiepval.	O'Reilly Lieut-Colonel Comdg 8th Bn R. I. Rifles.
	2.			
	3.		Hd. Qrs, C. & D. Coys in Martinsart.	
	4.		Inspections and refitting.	
	5.		29th Div. made a successful raid on enemy trenches. (THIEPVAL WOOD)	
	6.		Bn went into trenches and relieved 9th R. I. Rifles, 15th R. I. Rifles on left; 2nd Inniskillings on right.	
	7.		In Trenches. Very wet.	
	8.		" "	
	9.		Quiet day. Enemy artillery active at night.	
	10.		Heavy bombardment of enemy lines on enemy raid on the batt lines on our left. 8/12723 Cpl W. J. Dickson, 17/603 Rfm J. Close, 9/12406 Rfm W. J. Quinn, 14/6513 Rfm W. Steele, and 17/707 Rfm D. Kirkpatrick killed about midnight. 2nd Lt. R. McB. Pettigrew, 8/12581 Sgt J. Boyd, 17/14441 Rfm J. McCarthy, & 11/1039 Rfm W. Jamson seriously wounded by shrapnel. Lieut. G. R. Moginety, 5/16650 Cpl W. Kirkpatrick, 8/12528 Cpl J. Atkinson, 8/12374 Rfm J. Black, 5/12760 Rfm K. Boyce, 8/13158 Rfm K. McIntosh, 5/6444 Rfm R. Lowry, 8/12489 Rfm J. Reid, 17/1352 Rfm K. Boyd, 8/3698 Rfm H. Cairnduff and 17/1090 Rfm S. Mullan wounded by shrapnel. 2nd Lt. A. J. Walshe wounded (shell shock)	
	11		2nd Lt. R. McB. Pettigrew, 8/12581 Sgt J. Boyd, 17/14441 Rfm J. McCarthy, and 11/1039 Rfm W. Jamson died of wounds.	
	12		8/11099 Rfm W. Boland killed. 8/13762 L/C C. Lance wounded (shell shock)	
	13.		Quiet day. Relieved by 9th R. I. Rifles and marched to billets in Martinsart. Hd. Qrs, "A" & "B" Coys in support to 9th R. I. Rifles. "C" & "D" Coys remained in billets. Lieut G. R. Moginety died of wounds. Capt. J. D. Nicholl slightly wounded.	
	14			

WAR DIARY or INTELLIGENCE SUMMARY

Army Form C. 2118.

(Erase heading not required.)

Instructions regarding War Diaries and Intelligence Summaries are contained in F.S. Regs., Part II. and the Staff Manual respectively. Title pages will be prepared in manuscript.

Place	Date	Hour	Summary of Events and Information	Remarks and references to Appendices
On Service.	15		Supplied working parties on assembly trenches, Shelwal.	J.T. Kelly Lieut-Colonel Comdg 8th Bn. C.G. Rifles
	16		- do -	
	17		- do -	
	18		8/13424 L/Cpl D. Robson, 8/12841 Rfn W. Gray, 17/1061 Rfn S. Green, 17/1537 Rfn B. Harron, 17/1592 Rfn W.J. Hamilton and 17/1146 Rfn S.G. Turner wounded.	
	19		Working parties on assembly trenches.	
	20		Relieved 9th Bn R.I. Rifles in trenches, A'B' & 'C' Coys in front line, 'D' Coy in reserve. 15th H.L.I. on right, 12th R.I. Rifles on left.	
	21		8/15592 Rfn J. Millar killed. 8/12898 Rfn R. Hutton, 8/13589 Rfn J. Shields, 17/641 Rfn B. Savage, 9/17002 Rfn R. Shields, 8/12516 Sgt W.B. Anderson, 8/13039 Rfn D. Lowry, 8/12768 Rfn D. Ferguson, 8/12463 Rfn W.J. Wilson, 8/12452 Rfn D. Walker and 8/11051 Rfn J. Bailie wounded.	
	22		'A' 'B' Coys relieved by 9th Innis Fus and marched to billets in Varennes.	
	23		'B' & 'C' " - do -	
	24		Cleaning equipment, inspections, etc.,	
	25			
	26		Practice attacks over rough ground, showing German trenches near CLAIR FAYE	
	27		Bn Balls moved to Hedauville.	
	28			
	29		In Hedauville	
	30		The Balls marched to Shelwy Wood and took up position in assembly trenches.	

1577 Wt.W10791/1773 50,000 1/15 D D & L A.D.S.S./Forms/C. 2118.

107th Brigade.
36th Division.

1/8th BATTALION

ROYAL IRISH RIFLES.

JULY 1916::

WAR DIARY
or
INTELLIGENCE SUMMARY.

Army Form C. 2118.

36/ July
8/R.I.R 8
Vol 8

Place	Date	Hour	Summary of Events and Information	Remarks and references to Appendices
	July 1st 16		The Battalion reached assembly trenches AVELUY WOOD about 10.30 p.m. Tea was issued to the men. At dawn stores and bombs were issued to companies, we were shelled intermittently but suffered no casualties.	
		5 am	Batt. marched from AVELUY WOOD to a position at Speyside, THIEPVAL WOOD and remained there during the intensive bombardment which lasted 1¼ hours. The Batt. behaved remarkably well during the bombardment. Our casualties while at Speyside were 8 killed and 15 wounded.	
		7.30 am	Batt. marched from Speyside to ELGIN AVENUE, and up the ride to NO. MAN'S LAND, picking up R.E. stores en route at GORDON CASTLE, THIEPVAL WOOD. Deployed in NO MAN'S LAND and advanced in rear of 9" R.I. Rifles, while marching along Speyside a group of German prisoners were marched past us, this made the men more enthusiastic than ever, if that were possible.	
		9.40 am	German "B" Line was reached (reference 10" Bopr. Special map) and numerous prisoners captured. Direction was lost and the Battalion found itself too far to the left. This was corrected during next advance.	
		10.10 am	Reached "C" Line and moved straight on & laid down between the "C" and "D" Lines. Entered "D" Line trenches, the barrage having lifted. Heavy casualties occurred during the advance from "C" to "D" Line owing to enfilade Machine Gun fire from BEAUCOURT REDOUBT and Machine Gun and Rifle Fire almost in reverse from THIEPVAL.	
		11. am		

WAR DIARY
or
INTELLIGENCE SUMMARY.
(Erase heading not required.)

Army Form C. 2118.

Place	Date	Hour	Summary of Events and Information	Remarks and references to Appendices
	1.7.16	11 a.m.	"D" Line was entered at Point D.9.	
		11.9 a.m.	Barrage shortened and made D Line untenable. Battalion therefore returned to between "D" and "C" Lines. As many of our shells were falling short, the battalion retired to C Line and took up the line L.9., B.10 and C.11. Capt. J.J. McCallum reconnoitred the S.E. face of SCHWABEN REDOUBT, and found some of the 9th R.S. Rifles at B.14 under Major Gaffikin. He then worked to the right and found Lieut Sanderson and 2 Machine Guns of 107th Bde Machine Gun Coy. at 68. The Lieut Sanderson to reconnoitre towards THIEPVAL. Lieut Sanderson worked down trench running from R.20.c.8.2. to R.26.a.2.3. and at the latter point encountered the enemy, and ascertained that THIEPVAL was in their hands. He then returned and reported to Capt. McCallum.	
		12.6 p.m.	Trenches from midway between B.11 and B.10 to B.10, the S.E. face of SCHWABEN REDOUBT, from B.10 nearly to B.14, and also the trench running N.E. from C.9 along the THIEPVAL—GRANDCOURT ROAD were heavily shelled by heavy guns from the N.E. and rendered untenable. Heavy casualties occurred and the Battalion was withdrawn to the line B.14 - B.13 - B.15, with the exception of a party that remained holding C.11.	
		12.30 p.m.	Garrison of C.8 and trench between C.8 and B.14 withdrawn to the triangle B.13, B.14, B.15, by order of Major Gaffikin. Capt. McCallum then finding the men too thick in this triangle distributed the men of the 8th R.J. Rifles to the N.W. face of SCHWABEN REDOUBT and	

Army Form C. 2118.

WAR DIARY
or
INTELLIGENCE SUMMARY.
(Erase heading not required.)

Instructions regarding War Diaries and Intelligence Summaries are contained in F. S. Regs., Part II. and the Staff Manual respectively. Title pages will be prepared in manuscript.

Place	Date	Hour	Summary of Events and Information	Remarks and references to Appendices
	1.7.16	12.30pm	consolidated the line between B18 and B11.	
		1.55pm	Capt. McCallum found that there was a shortage of bombs and sent to ask for a fresh supply.	
		3.30pm	Enemy (about half battalion) emerged from trees in R.13. d.8.8. and advanced against B.11. Our artillery however got on to them and practically wiped them out.	
		3.50pm	Enemy made three bombing attacks. (1) Along trench running along GRANDCOURT - THIEPVAL ROAD from D10, which was driven off on reaching R.20. b.27. (2) From B.12 to B.11 which was driven back by 2/Lieut T.J. Allen, 8th Bn. R.I. Rifles who bombed them right back to B.12 single-handed. He was killed about 10 minutes after his return to B.11. (3) From trench running from R.14. c.4 & 5. to R.20. a.5.9. (This trench runs from there to B.15 although not shown on the map.) This attack worked along as far as R.19. d.6.7. when it came in contact with a blocking party of ours. But the enemy outranged our men with his handle bombs and things were looking bad when Lieut Sanderson 107th Bde. M.G. Coy. collected 8 or 9 men at B.13 and charged across the open. Lieut. Sanderson was killed. 2nd Lieut. Brown 8th Bn. R.I. Rifles also took a party from R.19. b.6.1. and bombed the trench where enemy bombers were, and no more annoyance was caused. 2nd Lieut. Brown who was wounded.	J.G. Smith Major Comdg 8th Bn R. I. Rifles

WAR DIARY
or
INTELLIGENCE SUMMARY.
(Erase heading not required.)

Army Form C. 2118.

Place	Date	Hour	Summary of Events and Information	Remarks and references to Appendices
	1/7/16	4.45 pm	Two more bombing attacks were made by the enemy against C.11 from C.12. both of which were driven off. About this time our guns opened fire on the trenches near C.11 and it was noticed that some troops in the "B" line were displaying their yellow flags. Our contact aeroplane came over very low and our yellow flags were shown and flares burnt, and soon the shelling ceased.	
		7.15 pm	Enemy's heavy guns heavily bombarded the triangle B.13 - B.14 - B.15 for an hour.	
		8.30 pm	Capt. McCallum and Sgt. Lowry went to investigate and worked along from B.17 - B.15 - B.13 - B.14 to B.16 and found trenches unoccupied. An enemy bombing attack was heard near C.9 or C.apt. McCallum and Sgt. Lowry returned to B.17. He found none in the "B" line and as his party at C.11 was dangerously isolated he withdrew them and established himself on the line A.14, A.15, A.16, A.17, where they found a party of between 20 and 30 men under Lieut Stewart (107th Cole. M.g. Coy.) There the Battalion reorganised, a blocking party put out to the left and a patrol sent out to reconnoitre to the right. The patrol returned after half an hour, and reported having found no men	

Army Form C. 2118.

WAR DIARY
or
INTELLIGENCE SUMMARY.
(Erase heading not required.)

Instructions regarding War Diaries and Intelligence Summaries are contained in F. S. Regs., Part II. and the Staff Manual respectively. Title pages will be prepared in manuscript.

Place	Date	Hour	Summary of Events and Information	Remarks and references to Appendices
	1/7/16	8.30pm	of either side for a considerable distance.	
		10pm.	Several enemy bombing attacks were launched from the neighbourhood of the CRUCIFIX and a strong one from THIEPVAL which came in contact with our blocking party at A.14. We only had about 12 bombs left, but these sufficed to drive off this attack.	
		10.20pm	Another bombing attack came from THIEPVAL working up both "A" front and support lines. Having no bombs and very little ammunition left our men withdrew to the "A" front line, South of A.14 to A.15 to avoid being cut off. Here 100 men of the W. Yorks were found, who had ammunition but no bombs and no water.	
		10.45pm	For the next half hour or so about 100 men came in, in twos and threes from various points, who were collected and reorganised.	
		11.15pm	Strong parties of enemy were found to be collecting near the CRUCIFIX and B.17. 2 or 3 red flares were fired for artillery support, but without result.	
		11.30pm	Several bombing patrols approached which were driven off with rifle fire.	

Conveys S.R. Coy. O. i/c Coys.
Major
[signature]

WAR DIARY
or
INTELLIGENCE SUMMARY.

(Erase heading not required.)

Army Form C. 2118.

Place	Date	Hour	Summary of Events and Information	Remarks and references to Appendices
	1/7/16	11.45 PM	Having practically no ammunition left it was decided to withdraw to our lines and the men were divided up into five parties which were led independently across to our lines	
		12.15 AM	3 officers and about 100 men returned with these parties	
	July 2nd	12 noon	Received orders to place all available officers and men under orders of Lt-Col Turgen, 9th C.I.B., who was to command a mixed force and reoccupy the A Line from A.15 to A.19. 9 officers and 120 men were sent	
		1.30 PM	The party left Gordon Castle. The Battalion reached the A Line with about 15 casualties. Consolidation proceeded without hindrance. Several bombing attacks were driven off. Our patrols went almost to St. Pierre Divion.	
	3/7/16	2 AM	First party relieved by W. Yorks.	
		8 AM	Remainder of Battalion relieved.	
General Remarks			The enemy's wire was at the D. Line was well cut in places. Our artillery fire had no effect on the enemy's deep dug-outs although the trenches were smashed	

WAR DIARY
or
INTELLIGENCE SUMMARY.

(Erase heading not required.)

Army Form C. 2118.

Place	Date	Hour	Summary of Events and Information	Remarks and references to Appendices
General Remarks			Our men although carrying no packs complained of being too heavily loaded. The assaulting columns should go into action as light as possible. The carrying of R.E. stores by the assaulting troops was not a success. Most of these in the test of battle, were dropped and lost. It would be better to send them up afterwards. The trenches should be carefully cleared before advancing beyond them. In many cases Germans surrendered and when our men went on without leaving sufficient escort, the surrendered enemy fetched Machine Guns out of Dug-outs, and fired into our men's backs. Parties of Germans advanced up trenches with their hands up as if surrendering but in reality acted as a screen to hide bombing parties behind them. The use of flags to denote the most advanced infantry, is dangerous, as it is difficult to ensure them not being displayed in rear. The contact aeroplanes were very useful and communication between them and the ground should be perfected.	Major Loring 8.13. R.g. Rifles

Army Form C. 2118.

WAR DIARY
or
INTELLIGENCE SUMMARY.
(Erase heading not required.)

Instructions regarding War Diaries and Intelligence Summaries are contained in F. S. Regs., Part II. and the Staff Manual respectively. Title pages will be prepared in manuscript.

Place	Date	Hour	Summary of Events and Information	Remarks and references to Appendices
	General Remarks		Telephones were quite useless further forward than Battalion H.qrs. The importance of every man knowing his particular task cannot be overestimated. So many cases during the advance the men carried on, though they had lost their officers and N.C.O.'s Deep dug outs on the German plan, in our trenches would have save many casualties. Without these and the strong Machine Gun Emplacements attacked, the village of THIEPVAL could not have held out, and prevented our success after our tough bombardment. German handle bombs outranged ours by several yards, but ours were more accurately thrown. Lewis Guns were particularly useful in supporting bombing & blocking parties. Also Lewis Gun magazines in a bucket is too heavy a load.	Casualties 8/13 R. Rifle...
			Casualties Killed .... Off. — O.R. 24 (2 Off. shell shock)	
			Wounded .... 13 197 (1× shell shock)	
			Wounded (at duty) .... 2 19 (3 shell shock)	
			Missing 2 176	
			Missing believed wounded ... 1 8	
			Missing believed killed 2 2	

Army Form C. 2118.

WAR DIARY
or
INTELLIGENCE SUMMARY.
(Erase heading not required.)

Instructions regarding War Diaries and Intelligence Summaries are contained in F. S. Regs., Part II. and the Staff Manual respectively. Title pages will be prepared in manuscript.

Place	Date	Hour	Summary of Events and Information	Remarks and references to Appendices
	4/7/16		Battalion marched to Harponville via HEDAUVILLE – VARENNES.	
	5/7/16		The 109th Brigade was inspected by G.O.C. 36th Divr. (General Nugent) The paid glowing tribute to the work of the Brigade on July 1st & 2nd 1916. Batt left HARPONVILLE and marched to RUBEMPRE VIA TOUTENCOURT – HERRISART.	
	6/7/16		Bay. inspection. Received orders to be ready to move at 3/4 hour notice.	
	7/7/16		3/4 hour notice to move raised to 2 hours. Took the Batt. to a variety performance named the TYKES.	
	8/7/16		Received orders to be ready to move on the 9.7.'16. this move was eventually cancelled.	
	9/7/16		Divine Service in the morning, in the evening we had the Drums playing for 1 hour which the men thoroughly enjoyed.	
	10/7/16	6 a.m.	Batt marched to BERNAVILLE. Day was very hot, but we completed the march without any men falling out.	
	11/7/16		Left BERNAVILLE and marched to AUXI-LE-CHATEAU, entrained here and went to THIENNES, marched from there to WARDRECQUES VIA BOESEGHEM – WITTES – RACQUENGHEM, we arrived at our billet after a very hard day about 11 p.m.	

Army Form C. 2118.

WAR DIARY
or
INTELLIGENCE SUMMARY.
(Erase heading not required.)

Instructions regarding War Diaries and Intelligence Summaries are contained in F. S. Regs., Part II. and the Staff Manual respectively. Title pages will be prepared in manuscript.

Place	Date	Hour	Summary of Events and Information	Remarks and references to Appendices
	12.7.16		Clearing of billets, giving the men as much rest as possible.	Casualty 6 O.R. & 5 Light
	13.7.16		Marched to BAYENGHEM, VIA ARQUES – ST. OMER – ST. MARTIN – TILQUES – MOULLE. Hard march but the men had very good billets. A draft of 54 other ranks arrived from 17th and 19th Batt. K.R. Rifles, quite a smart lot of men.	
	14.7.16		We moved 6 "D" boys to new billets at OEUST MONT and kept H.Q. A & B boys at BAYENGHEM. General cleaning up and resting.	
	15.7.16		Batt. parade in morning. Divine service in the morning. C.O. inspected draft that arrived on the 13.7.16 at 2.30pm. Draft arrived from Base. Strength 26, of these mostly men who were wounded on 1st or 2nd July '16.	
	16.7.16		Batt. parades in morning.	
	17.7.16		Bay. parades in morning. Batt. parade in the afternoon.	
	18.7.16		Bay. parades in morning. Batt. parade in the afternoon. C.O. inspected the draft that arrived on the 16.7.'16	
	19.7.16		Batt. had a short route march. Bathed in river just outside BAYENGHEM.	
	20.7.16		Batt. marched to MERCHENGHEM, VIA WATTEN.	
	21.7.16		Marched to WORMHOUDT. VIA. BOLLEZEELE – ZEGGERS – CAPPEL – ESQUELBECQ.	

WAR DIARY
or
INTELLIGENCE SUMMARY
(Erase heading not required.)

Army Form C. 2118.

Place	Date	Hour	Summary of Events and Information	Remarks and references to Appendices
	22.7.16		Marched to HONDIGEN, via CASSEL – ST. MARIE CAPPEL. Draft of 61 other ranks arrived from 3rd Batt. R.I. Rifles, a good stamp of men.	
	23.7.16		Marched to STEENWERCK VIA BORRE – STRAZELLE. A hot day and a trying march.	
	24.7.16		Cleaning up billets, equipment etc.	
	25.7.16		Coy parades and instructional classes.	
	26.7.16		Batt. had baths at STEENWERCK in the morning. Coy Bombing and Bayonet fighting parades in the afternoon.	
	27.7.16		Marched to a camp at KORTEPYP. Found a carrying party for the trenches, 6 officers, 20 N.C.O.'s and 304 other ranks. Carrying all night, arrived back in camp at 6 A.M. 28.7.1916.	
	28.7.16		A very quiet day. The men slept all morning, the afternoon was devoted to Coy. Bomberis parades.	
	29.7.16		Coy. parades. Bomb-throwing competition in the afternoon.	
	30.7.16		Divine Service in the morning. Bomb throwing & Bayonet fighting in the afternoon. Visited the line that Batt. was to take over on Monday the 31st.	
	31.7.16		Preparing to move out to the trenches. Batt inspected by the C.O. General turn out of the men very good. Batt moved out for the trenches by Platoons at 5 minute intervals at 8.35 pm. Relief carried out without any deviation from the usual programme. The Batt. line is T.1.B. 3.1. to T.6. 13.5.4. Maps R.J. sheet 28. S.W.(4). With the 1/5 Bn. Royal Irish Rifles on our right and the 6th Bn. Northumberland Fus. on our left.	

1577. Wt.W19791/1773 500,000 1/15 D.D.& L. A.P.S.S.(Forms)C. 2118.

Page 1.
8th Bn K.S. Rifles

WAR DIARY
or
INTELLIGENCE SUMMARY

Army Form C. 2118.

8th R.I.R. Vol 9

W. Whitehouse Lt:Col.
Comdg 8th Bn K.R.R.Rifles

Place	Date	Hour	Summary of Events and Information	Remarks and references to Appendices
In the Trenches	1/8/16		A quiet day.	
"	2/8/16		Very quiet during the morning. In the afternoon the enemy staffed the Batt. on our left (6th Northumberland Fus.) with Trench Mortars; no damage to our line	
"	3/8/16		In the afternoon the enemy bombarded our line with Trench Mortars, very little damage to our line, but had casualties to the extent of 1 Officer, 3 O.R. Wounded and 1 Officer 20 O.R. wounded (shell shock)	
"	4/8/16		13 Coy. Left Coy. had a bad time yesterday and we relieved them with A. Coy. B.Coy. coming back to support at BARBERRY COAST. 13 Coy. about 800 yards behind the front line. Batt. on our left staffed with French Mortars. We had one casualty, 1 O.R. killed by sniper	
"	5/8/16		Very quiet during morning, but in the afternoon the enemy bombarded our line with French Mortars, this lasted about 1 hour, no damage and no casualties. Divisional front moved to the left. The 9th Bn. R.I. Rifles came in on our left, with the 11th Bn. R.I. Rifles on our right. Batt. line now is M.1.A.4.5.15 to T.6.B.4.0.40. Map PLOEGSTEERT.	
"	6/8/16		Very quiet all day, sent a patrol out at 9.30 p.m. to try and catch one of the enemy, but did not succeed. patrol returned about 1.30 A.M. (7.8.16)	
"	7/8/16		About 8.30 A.M. enemy bombarded with 5.9, but no damage, & no casualties	

Page 2.
8th Bn. Royal Irish Rifles

Army Form C. 2118.

WAR DIARY
or
INTELLIGENCE SUMMARY.
(Erase heading not required.)

8 R I R

Bomds 84 Bn. R. I. R. B.
R.G. Hamilton
Lt.Col.

Place	Date	Hour	Summary of Events and Information	Remarks and references to Appendices
In the Trenches	7/8/16		In the afternoon he started his now usual bombardment with Trench Mortars, but as usual was soon quieted by our guns. No damage and no casualties	
"	8/8/16		Gas alarm passed along from the left at 8.20 am., turned out to be a false alarm. Naval Trench Mortar bombardment at 2.50 p.m. Our artillery extremely good, and soon quieted the enemy. No damage & no casualties. At 11 p.m. relieved by the 15th Bn. R. I. Rifles. We went back to billets at KORTEPYP. Billets of huts and tents.	
In Billets	9/8/16		A day of rest. Cleaning equipment, arms etc	
"	10/8/16		Coy parades in morning. Bombing in the afternoon.	
"	11/8/16		Coy parades in morning. Bayonet fighting & Bombing in the afternoon.	
"	12/8/16		Coy parades in morning. Bayonet fighting & bombing competition in the afternoon.	
"	13/8/16		Church parade in morning. Lectures by Coy bomb[er]s in the afternoon.	
"	14/8/16		Route march by Coys. The King visited the Div. H.Q., each Batt. had to send representatives. Capt. J. D. McCallum and Sgt. McWilliam represented the 8th Bn. party inspected by His Majesty.	
"	15/8/16		Coy parades in the morning. Lectures on "Gas Attack" by Coy. bomb[er]s in the afternoon.	
"	16/8/16		Getting ready to go into the trenches. Very quiet day. At 9.30 p.m. relieved the 15th Bn. R. I. Rifles with 13 + D. Coys in the line, L Coy at BARBERRY COAST, + A Coy in FORBES TERRACE. A very good relief. The 9th Bn R. I. Rifles on our left, + 11th Bn. R. I. Rifles on our right	

Page 3.
8th Bn. Royal Irish Rifles

Army Form C. 2118.

WAR DIARY
or
INTELLIGENCE SUMMARY.
(Erase heading not required.)

Place	Date	Hour	Summary of Events and Information	Remarks and references to Appendices
In the Trenches.	17/8/16		Very quiet day. Weather showery	
	18/8/16		Very quiet day. Weather fair	
	19/8/16		Very quiet up to about 10.30 A.M., when the enemy started the usual game with Trench Mortars, but no damage & no casualties. The enemy started his Trench Mortar again about 5pm and kept it up till about 5.45pm. Our Artillery was very busy, no damage and no casualties. About 9.30pm. 10R. Killed by rifle Grenade	
	20/8/16		About 12.30 A.M. Enemy Aeroplane crossed our lines, went in the direction of BAILLEUL & returned about 1.15 A.M. he was fired on by our Anti-Aircraft Guns, could not observe effect. Very quiet up to about 5pm. when we had the usual French Mortar Bombardment for ½ of an hour, no damage & no casualties	
	21/8/16		Very quiet up to about 3.45pm, when the Trench Mortars started for about 1 hour. Our Artillery were very busy, no damage & no casualties. 11th Bn. 6 R.I. Rifles the Batt. on our right relieved by the 12th Bn. R.I. Rifles	
	22/8/16		Quiet in the morning, but enemy had his usual bombardment in the afternoon, a little damage done to trenches but no casualties	
	23/8/16		Very quiet during morning and afternoon, but in the evening about 6pm. the enemy again started on our front line with Trench Mortars & Heavies 5.9. No damage & no casualties.	
	24/8/16		Morel calm during morning, but very lively in the afternoon. The enemy shelling our front line with Whizz Bangs and Trench Mortars, our Artillery retaliated by knocking in part of the Enemy's parapet	

Lt-Col.
P.J. Alexander
Comdg. 8th Bn. R.I. Rifles

WAR DIARY or INTELLIGENCE SUMMARY.

Army Form C. 2118.

8th Bn Royal Irish Rifles

Page 4

Place	Date	Hour	Summary of Events and Information	Remarks and references to Appendices
In the Trenches.	24/8/16		We were relieved about 11 p.m. by the 15th Bn R.I. Rifles. A very good relief. We marched to billets just outside NEUVE EGLISE, Bn. Hq. at T.9.D.60.30. A & C Coys at T.H.C.70.50. B & D Coys at T.10.C.98.90. Very bad billets.	G R Collins-Walter Lt-Col Comdg 8th Bn R.I. Rifles
In Billets.	25/8/16		Quiet day. Men resting & cleaning as much as possible.	
"	26/8/16		Lectures by Company Comdgs during morning. In the evening found working party of 8 Officers, 14. N.C.O's & 231 other ranks, to carry Roger Cylinders to the front line. Trench C.3. Drums played for half an hour to each double Coy in billets. Drums played for half an hour to each double Coy which the men greatly appreciated.	
"	27/8/16		At night we found working party of 8 Officers, 14. N.C.O's & 231 other ranks, to carry Roger Cylinders to Trench C.H.	
"	28/8/16		Morning. Lectures by Coy. Commanders. In the evening we found working parties for the front line etc. 7 Officers and 240 other ranks.	
"	29/8/16		Lectures by Platoon commanders. In the evening Batt. was to have found working party of 7 Officers and 240 O.Ranks, but owing to heavy rain it was cancelled.	
"	30/8/16			
"	31/8/16		Lectures by Instr. Staff N.C.O's in the morning. Working parties of 7 Officers and 240 O.Ranks in the evening.	

Vol 10

8th Bn. Royal Irish Rifles.   September 1916.

WAR DIARY
INTELLIGENCE SUMMARY
(Erase heading not required.)

Army Form C. 2118.

Place	Date	Hour	Summary of Events and Information	Remarks and references to Appendices
	1-9-16		Cleaning up during the day. At 8.30 p.m. started to relieve the 15th Bn. R.I. Rifles in the line. A very good relief. 11th Bn. R.I. Rifles on our right with 9th Bn. R.I. Rifles on our left.	
	2-9-16		In the Trenches. A very quiet day.	
	3-9-16		In the Trenches. A very quiet day.	
	4-9-16		In the Trenches. A very quiet day. 11th Bn. R.I. Rifles on our right relieved by the 12th Bn. R.I. Rifles.	
	5-9-16		In the Trenches. A very quiet day, at about 10 p.m. our Artillery bombarded a sector of Enemy's Trenches at N36.A.8.7. N36.A.6.6. with a view to the 57th Bde. making a raid.	
	6-9-16		Very quiet during the morning. Our Artillery bombarded a sector of the Enemy's Trenches at N.36.D.70.05 - N.36.D.57.40. from 3 p.m. to about 3.50 p.m. Very quiet on our sector. Our Artillery bombarded the Enemy's Communications from 10 p.m. to 1 a.m. and 3 a.m. to 6 a.m. No retaliation.	
	7-9-16		Great aeroplane activity. Artillery shelled the Enemy's 1st Line & Communications.	
	8-9-16		In the Trenches. A very quiet day. About 8.30 p.m. a Gas Alarm was sounded, starting up north, probably YPRES, it turned out to be a false alarm.	

J.C. Hamilton   Lt. Col.
Commanding 8th Bn. R. I. Rifles.

WAR DIARY
INTELLIGENCE SUMMARY

8th Bn. Royal Irish Rifles. September 1916. Army Form C. 2118.

Instructions regarding War Diaries and Intelligence Summaries are contained in F. S. Regs., Part II. and the Staff Manual respectively. Title pages will be prepared in manuscript.

(Erase heading not required.)

Place	Date	Hour	Summary of Events and Information	Remarks and references to Appendices
	9-9-16		Quiet day in trenches. Relieved by 15th Bn. Royal Irish Rifles and proceeded to KORTEPYP CAMP.	
	10-9-16		Sunday. In billets. Divine Services of the following denominations held:- Presbyterian, Church of Ireland and Roman Catholic.	
	11-9-16		In billets. Bathing carried out.	
	12-9-16		In billets. Working parties supplied consisting of 1 Off. & N.C.O.'s & 60 men. Instruction in Rapid Wiring and Sand-bag revetting. Fitting men small box respirators.	
	13-9-16		In billets. Working parties supplied consisting of 1 Off. & N.C.O.'s & 60 men. Battalion Medical Inspection.	
	14-9-16		In billets. Working parties supplied consisting of 1 Off. & N.C.O.'s & 60 men. Instruction in Rapid Wiring and Sand-bag revetting.	
	15-9-16		In billets. Working parties supplied consisting of 1 Off. & N.C.O.'s & 60 men.	
	16-9-16		In billets. Working parties supplied consisting of 1 Off. & N.C.O.'s & 60 men.	
	17-9-16		In billets. Divine Service. Relieved 15th Bn. Royal Irish Rifles in the trenches.	
	18-9-16		In the trenches. A very quiet day. 12th Bn. R.I. Rifles on our right, & 9th Bn. R. Rifles on our left.	

WAR DIARY

8th Bn. Royal Irish Rifles.

September 1916.

Army Form C. 2118.

(Erase heading not required.)

Instructions regarding War Diaries and Intelligence Summaries are contained in F. S. Regs., Part II. and the Staff Manual respectively. Title pages will be prepared in manuscript.

Place	Date	Hour	Summary of Events and Information	Remarks and references to Appendices
	19.9.16		In the trenches. A very quiet day.	
	20.9.16		In the trenches. Very quiet morning. During the afternoon the enemy artillery was active, we replied with Trench Mortars.	
	21.9.16		In the trenches. Morning again quiet. Artillery active on both sides during the afternoon.	
	22.9.16		In the trenches. Very quiet morning. During the afternoon our trench mortars medium and stokes, screened by 18 pdrs and 4.5 hows. bombarded the enemy front line. Enemy retaliation very weak.	
	23.9.16		In the Trenches. Very quiet day. Relieved by 15th Bn. R.I. Rifles and proceeded to billets at NEUVE EGLISE.	
	24.9.16		In billets. Divine Service held at Company billets.	
	25.9.16		In billets. Supplied working parties to extent of 4 Off. and 180 O.R.s Bathing was also carried out.	
	26.9.16		In billets. Supplied working parties to extent of 4 Off. and 180 O.R.s Bathing was also carried out.	
	27.9.16		In billets. Supplied working parties to extent of 4 Off. and 180 O.R.s Bathing was also carried out.	

J. Colt Hamilton Lt. Col.
Commanding 8th Bn. R.I. Rifles.

Army Form C. 2118.

8th Bn. Royal Irish Rifles.   September, 1916.

WAR DIARY

INTELLIGENCE SUMMARY.

(Erase heading not required.)

Place	Date	Hour	Summary of Events and Information	Remarks and references to Appendices
	28.9.16		In billets. Working parties to the extent of 2 Off. and 110 O.R's supplied. Bathing also carried out.	
	29.9.16		In billets. Lectures under Coy. arrangements during morning. In the evening relieved the 15th Bn. R.I. Rifles in the Trenches. A very good relief. 12th Bn. Royal Irish Rifles on our Right & 9th Bn. Royal Irish Rifles on our Left.	
	30.9.16		In the Trenches. A very quiet day, nothing unusual happened.	

C.H.Alexander Lt-Col.
Commanding 8th Bn. R.I. Rifles.

8th Bn. Royal Irish Rifles.

WAR DIARY

or

INTELLIGENCE SUMMARY.

(Erase heading not required.)

Army Form C. 2118.

October '16

Place	Date	Hour	Summary of Events and Information	Remarks and references to Appendices
In the Trenches.	1-10-16.		Very quiet day. weather wet and miserable.	
In the Trenches.	2-10-16.		Very quiet day. weather wet and miserable.	
In the Trenches.	3-10-16.		Our Trench Mortars carried out a bombardment in the morning for about ½ an hour; very little retaliation. Brigade consented to an issue of Rum, owing to the bad weather. The men greatly appreciated this.	
In the Trenches.	4-10-16.		Very quiet during morning, but about 3pm and 7.30 pm the Bosh bombarded our trenches with 5.9 and Trench Mortars, each bombardment lasting about 35 minutes. Very little damage done, 2 casualties slightly wounded.	
In the Trenches.	5-10-16.		At 8.30 a.m. our Artillery and Trench Mortars opened a bombardment on enemy's line, 10 minutes bombardment + 10 minutes interval for 1 hour and 5 minutes. Relieved in the line by the 15th Bn. Royal Irish Rifles. The Batt. marched to Billets at KORTEPYP.	
In Billets.	6-10-16.		Day devoted to cleaning equipment and kit inspection.	
In Billets.	7-10-16.		Morning. Divisional Baths allotted to the Battalion. Afternoon steady drill and Grenade practice.	
In Billets.	8-10-16.		Divine Service. In the afternoon the Drums played	

8th Bn. Royal Irish Rifles.   WAR DIARY   October '16.   Army Form C. 2118.

INTELLIGENCE SUMMARY.

(Erase heading not required.)

Place	Date	Hour	Summary of Events and Information	Remarks and references to Appendices
In Billets.	8-10-16		a selection for one hour, which the men greatly appreciated.	
In Billets.	9-10-16		Battalion parade 9.30 to 10.30 a.m. and 11.30 a.m. to 12.30 p.m. Bayonet fighting. Two to three p.m. Grenade Practice. 3 to 3.30 p.m. Lecture by Coy. Commanders.	
In Billets.	10-10-16		Battalion outing to BALLIEUL. Left billets at 12 noon, headed by the Battalion Drums, when about 1 mile out we were met by the Divisional Brass Band who with the Drums played to BALLIEUL. Arms were piled in a field just outside the town; and the men were marched to the Cinema Show and the Follies, from there to the 110th Field Ambulance where Tea was served. After tea the men were free to walk around the town until time for marching home. Arrived back in Billets about 8 p.m. A very successful outing, greatly appreciated by the men.	
In Billets.	11-10-16		Morning devoted to Kit Inspection and rubbing of feet, prior to move to Trenches. Relieved the 15th Bn. Royal Irish Rifles in the Line. A very good Relief, that was finished by 7 p.m.	

G.L.J. Howarden Lt. Col.
Comdg. 8th Bn. Royal Irish Rifles.

Army Form C. 2118.

8th Bn. Royal Irish Rifles. October, '16

WAR DIARY
INTELLIGENCE SUMMARY
(Erase heading not required.)

Instructions regarding War Diaries and Intelligence Summaries are contained in F.S. Regs, Part II. and the Staff Manual respectively. Title pages will be prepared in manuscript.

Place	Date	Hour	Summary of Events and Information	Remarks and references to Appendices
In the Trenches.	12.10.16		A fairly quiet day.	
In the Trenches.	13.10.16		A fairly quiet day.	
In the Trenches.	14.10.16		A fairly quiet day.	
In the Trenches.	15.10.16		A fairly quiet day.	
In the Trenches.	16.10.16		A fairly quiet day.	
In the Trenches.	17.10.16		Our Trench Mortars and Artillery bombarded the enemy's front for 1 hour and 5 minutes doing great damage. Very little retaliation. Battalion relieved by the 15th Bn. R.I.R. A good relief finished about 10 p.m. Went into billets near NEUVE EGLISE.	
In Billets.	18.10.16		Divisional Baths allotted to Battalion. Afternoon Arms and Kit Inspection.	
In Billets.	19.10.16		Working parties to the extent of 7 Officers and 188 O.R. for the Trenches	
In Billets.	20.10.16		Battalion found working parties for Trenches to the extent of 7 Officers and 188 O.R.	
In Billets.	21.10.16		Working parties for Trenches, but number increased to 7 Officers and 244 O.R.	

Lieut Colonel
Commdg 8th Bn. Royal Irish Rifles

Army Form C. 2118.

WAR DIARY
INTELLIGENCE SUMMARY
(Erase heading not required.)

Instructions regarding War Diaries and Intelligence Summaries are contained in F.S. Regs., Part II. and the Staff Manual respectively. Title pages will be prepared in manuscript.

8th Bn. Royal Irish Rifles.   October '16

Place	Date	Hour	Summary of Events and Information	Remarks and references to Appendices
In Billets	22.10.16		Found working parties for the Trenches, to the extent of 7 Officers and 244 O.R.	
In Billets	23.10.16		Morning devoted to rubbing of feet and kit inspection. Starting at 2pm, a very good relief finished by 5.5pm. Relieved the 15th Bn. R.I. Rifles in the trenches.	
In the Trenches	24.10.16		A fairly quiet day.	
In the Trenches	25.10.16		A fairly quiet day.	
In the Trenches	26.10.16		A fairly quiet day.	
In the Trenches	27.10.16		A fairly quiet day.	
In the Trenches	28.10.16		A fairly quiet day.	
In the Trenches	29.10.16		A fairly quiet day. Relieved in the Trenches by the 15th Bn. R.I. Rifles and proceeded to Rest Billets at KORTEPYP CAMP	
In Billets	30.10.16		Arms inspection and general cleaning of kit, equipment and huts etc. Working parties of 31 O.R. found.	
In Billets	31.10.16		Medical inspection; and inoculation of F. v. B. boys. Found working parties to the extent of 31 O.Ranks.	

(Sgd) E. Hamilton Lt. Col.
Comdg. 8th Bn. Royal Irish Rifles.

8th Bn. Royal Irish Rifles.   WAR DIARY   November 1916.   Army Form C. 2118.

Place	Date	Hour	Summary of Events and Information	Remarks and references to Appendices
	1-11-16		In Billets at KORTEPYP. Companies at drill during morning.	
	2-11-16		In the afternoon A Coy played C Coy at foot-ball, draw 1-1. In Billets. Field operations during morning. Bayonet fighting in the afternoon. Foot-ball. B Coy played D Coy and lost 2 to 0.	
	3-11-16		In Billets. Outing to BAILLEUL. Very successful day.	
	4-11-16		In Billets. Preparing to go to trenches. Kit inspection, etc.	
	5-11-16		In the trenches. Very quiet day.	
	6-11-16		In the trenches. Very quiet day. Lot of rain.	
	7-11-16		In the trenches. Very quiet day. Heavy rain and floods, the DOUVE overflowed its banks to a height of about 4 feet.	
	8-11-16		In the trenches. Very quiet day. Water began to drop.	
	9-11-16		In the trenches. Very quiet day. Water down.	
	10-11-16		In the trenches. Very quiet day. Relieved by the 15th Bn. R.I. Rifles, a very good relief. Completed by 5.30 p.m., withdrew to Billets at NEUVE EGLISE.	
	11-11-16		In Billets. Day devoted to bathing & Kit. Rifle & S.A.A. inspection.	
	12-11-16		In Billets. Found working parties for the Line, all available men	

8th Bn. Royal Irish Rifles.　　WAR DIARY　November, 1916.　Army Form C. 2118.

INTELLIGENCE SUMMARY.
(Erase heading not required.)

Place	Date	Hour	Summary of Events and Information	Remarks and references to Appendices
	13-11-'16		In Billets. All available men on working parties for the line.	
	14-11-'16		In Billets. All available men on working parties for the line.	
	15-11-'16		In Billets. All available men on working parties for the line.	
	16-11-'16		In Billets. Kit, Rifle & S.A.A. inspection. Rubbing of feet preparatory to going to trenches. Relieved 15th Bn. R.I. Rifles in the line; a very good relief completed by 5-5 p.m.	
	17-11-'16		In the Trenches. Very quiet day.	
	18-11-'16		In the Trenches. Very quiet day.	
	19-11-'16		In the Trenches. Fairly quiet day.	
	20-11-'16		In the Trenches. Fairly quiet day.	
	21-11-'16		In the Trenches. Quiet day.	
	22-11-'16		In the Trenches. Quiet day. Relieved by the 15th Bn. R.I. Rifles. Withdrew to billets at KORTEPYP. a good relief completed by 5-10 p.m.	
	23-11-'16		In Billets. Morning devoted to Kit, Rifle, and S.A.A. inspection. In the afternoon B.Coy played C.Coy and drew 5-5.	
	24-11-'16		In Billets. Bathing. Musketry; bayonet fighting.	

Remarks (top of page): J.C. Alexander Lt.-Col. Commdg. 8th Bn. Royal Irish Rifles.

8th Bn. Royal Irish Rifles. November, 1916. Army Form C. 2118.

WAR DIARY

(Erase heading not required.)

Place	Date	Hour	Summary of Events and Information	Remarks and references to Appendices
	25-11-'16		In billets. Coy. drill. Bayonet fighting. Musketry all morning. Physical Training in the afternoon. C.Coy. played D.Coy. and lost 2-0.	
	26-11-'16		In billets. Divine Service. The Drums played on the Square from 12. to 1 p.m. In the Afternoon A.Coy. played B.Coy. and lost 5-1.	
	27-11-'16		In billets. Coy. at drill. Musketry, bayonet fighting, and extended order drill etc. Last draft on the range. Afternoon. Lectures by Coy. Commanders.	
	28-11-'16		In billets. Preparing to go to trenches. Kit, Rifle v. S.A.A. inspection, also rubbing of feet. Relieved the 15th Bn. R. I. Rifles in the line. Very good relief; completed by 5.10 p.m.	
	29-11-'16		In the Trenches. Very quiet day.	
	30-11-'16		In the Trenches. Very quiet morning. At 2 p.m. our Trench Mortars, Light & Heavy, and Artillery bombarded the enemy's lines, doing great damage. Enemy's casualties must have been very heavy, the bombardment ceased about 3.30 p.m. Hostile retaliation very slight.	

8th Bn. Royal Irish Rifles.   Army Form C. 2118.

WAR DIARY
or
INTELLIGENCE SUMMARY.
(Erase heading not required.)

December 1916.

Vol/3

Place	Date	Hour	Summary of Events and Information	Remarks and references to Appendices
In the Trenches	1/12/16		Quiet day. Weather misty	
do	2/12/16		Fairly quiet day. Boche artillery busy. Our artillery made him close down. Weather misty	
do	3/12/16		Quiet day. Weather bad	
do	4/12/16		A fairly lively day. The Boche artillery appeared to be registering. He kept up intermittent shelling till dusk, our artillery returning the fire. Were relieved in the line by the 15th R.I. Rifles. A very good relief finished by 4.15 P.M. Battalion withdrew to Billets in SHANKILL HUTS, UGBROOKE FARM and NEUVE EGLISE.	
Billets	6/12/16		Day devoted to Bathing and, Rifles, S.A.A and kit inspection. Half an hour physical training in the afternoon	
do	7/12/16		Found Working Parties up to 237 for the front and support lines	
do	8/12/16		do. do. do.	
do	9/12/16		do. do. do.	

8th Bn. Royal Irish Rifles.   WAR DIARY or INTELLIGENCE SUMMARY.   Army Form C. 2118.   December, 1916.

Instructions regarding War Diaries and Intelligence Summaries are contained in F.S. Regs., Part II. and the Staff Manual respectively. Title pages will be prepared in manuscript.

(Erase heading not required.)

Place	Date	Hour	Summary of Events and Information	Remarks and references to Appendices
In Billets	10/12/16		Morning devoted to Rifles, S.A.A, Kit Inspection and rubbing of men's feet.	
			Afternoon. Moved into the line and relieved the 15th Bn. R.I. Rifles. We took over an extra two trenches, i.e. T6.4, T6.5. Two companies in the line. Two companies in Battalion Reserve. Every good relief completed by 4.20 pm.	
In the trenches	11/12/16		A fairly quiet day. The Boche a little more active than usual but our artillery closed him down.	
do	12/12/16		Lively day. Intermittent shelling by both sides all day. A mixture of snow and rain fell all the morning and well into the afternoon.	
do	13/12/16		Intermittent shelling on both sides all day. Otherwise quiet. Weather fair, little rain at night.	
do	14/12/16		Slight shelling throughout the day by both sides, otherwise very quiet. Weather - dull.	
do	15/12/16		Our artillery and trench mortars bombarded the enemy's line from 10.30 am to 11 am, doing great damage. Slight enemy retaliation. No damage to our line. Remainder of day quiet. Weather fair, rain at night.	

Signed J. Stewart Major
Comdg. 8th Bn. Royal Irish Rifles.

8th Bn. Royal Irish Rifles

Army Form C. 2118.

WAR DIARY
or
INTELLIGENCE SUMMARY.
(Erase heading not required.)

Instructions regarding War Diaries and Intelligence Summaries are contained in F. S. Regs., Part II. and the Staff Manual respectively. Title pages will be prepared in manuscript.

Place	Date	Hour	Summary of Events and Information	Remarks and references to Appendices
In the trenches	16/2/16		The Battalion was relieved by the 15th Bn R.I. Rifles. A good relief completed by 5.30 p.m. The Battalion withdrawn to new billets at WAKEFIELD HUTS, DRANOUTRE. Quite a nice change from KORTEPYP	
In Billets	17/2/16		Day devoted to cleaning up generally. Parade under Company Commanders. Afternoon - football	
do	18/2/16		Adjutant's parade - 9.30 a.m. C.O.'s parade 11 a.m. Afternoon devoted to cleaning up generally	
do	19/2/16		The Battalion marched to SHANKILL HUTS (NEUVE EGLISE) for an inspection by the C.I.C. Gen. Sir Douglas Haig. The Battalion worked beautifully. The C.O.I.C. was so pleased with the turn out and steadiness of the men that he thought he was inspecting a LINE Battalion. After inspection Battalion marched back to billets and afternoon devoted to amusements.	
do	20/2/16		Parades under Coy. Comdrs. Afternoon - football.	

Army Form C. 2118.

8th Bn Royal Irish Rifles

WAR DIARY
or
INTELLIGENCE SUMMARY.
(Erase heading not required.)

Instructions regarding War Diaries and Intelligence Summaries are contained in F.S. Regs., Part II. and the Staff Manual respectively. Title pages will be prepared in manuscript.

Place	Date	Hour	Summary of Events and Information	Remarks and references to Appendices
In Billets	22/12/15		Morning - Preparing to move into the line. Afternoon - Battalion moved into the line in relief of 13th R.I. Rifles. A very good relief, completed by 5.10 pm.	
In Trenches	23/12/15		A very quiet day. Gas was released on the Brigade front. Although a very heavy wind was blowing we think the gas kept down. Two patrols were sent out 2 hours after discharge of gas. One from our Battalion, one from the 9th R.I. Rifles on our left. The enemy were, however, standing-to so the patrol came back. We had one slight casualty, 1 Officer being slightly wounded.	
do	24/12/15		Hostile artillery active. Otherwise quiet day	
do	25/12/15		Hostile artillery active. Our artillery responded. About 5 pm the enemy opened fire on our batteries with 5.9 shells. He fired about 300 shells into one field in the vicinity of Brigade Headquarters (NEUVE EGLISE) doing no damage, remainder of day quiet.	
do	26/12/15		Quiet day	
do	27/12/15		Artillery of both sides active, otherwise quiet.	

2nd B. Royal Irish Rifles

Army Form C. 2118.

WAR DIARY
or
INTELLIGENCE SUMMARY.
(Erase heading not required.)

Instructions regarding War Diaries and Intelligence Summaries are contained in F. S. Regs., Part II. and the Staff Manual respectively. Title pages will be prepared in manuscript.

Place	Date	Hour	Summary of Events and Information	Remarks and references to Appendices
In trenches	29/12/15		A heavy fog hung over the land until the afternoon. Consequently a quiet day. Relieved by 15" B: R. I. Rifles in the line. Good relief, completed by 5.10 p.m. Batte: withdrew to Billets at SHANKILL HUTS and NEUVE EGLISE. The Montenegran order of Danilo 5th Class was presented to Capt. Thornton, Acting Adjutant of the Battalion, by Major-General O.S.W. Nugent the Corps Commander.	Major Lonsdale 8.4.13: 15" I. Rifles [signature]
In Billets	30/12/15		Day devoted to bathing and generally cleaning up. Battalion found working parties up to 263 O.Ranks for the line	do.
do.	31/12/15		do.	do.

SYSTEM FOR PUTTING OUT WIRE TRESTLES.

The party is divided into sections of 3 men each - one section to each bay of entanglement - the bays are about 15 yards long.

The stores for each bay are:-

1 Trestle.
1 Coil of French Wire.
12 Iron Staples.
2 coils of barbed wire 20 yards long (rolled on a stick).
1 Mallet.

The sections are extended along the front to be wired - each section 15 yards apart.

No.1 of each section carries the Trestle.
No.2　"　"　"　"　" French wire & Staples.
No.3　"　"　"　"　" 2 coils barbed wire and Mallet.

No.1 places the Trestle in position.

No.2, as soon as the Trestle is out, places one end of the French coil on to the Trestle and the runs the other end out to the next Trestle on the right and then pegs the wire down with staples.

No.3 entwines the barbed wire and No.1 helps him.

It is best to work to the right along the whole line, i.e., run the French wire out from the Trestle to the next one on the right.

Amended Copy

Operation Orders
by
Lt. Col. R. T. Pelly, D.S.O.
Comdg 8th Bn. R. I. Rifles.
16th January 1916.

№ 16

Secret.

1. To-morrow night (17th/18th) the right portion of our line from saps 1 to 4 inclusive will be advanced, a new trench being dug linking up those 4 sap heads.

The cutting line will be taped out in readiness to night and officers in charge of working parties shown the ground.

2. **Covering Party.** — A covering party consisting of 4 squads of 1 N.C.O. and 6 men each, the whole under the command of Lieut Murphy will work out to beyond the crest of Hawthorne Ridge, one squad starting out from each sap, so as to be in position at 5.30 p.m.

A report will be sent to No 3 sap when the covering party is in position.

This party will be relieved by a similar party under Lieut McGusty at 11 p.m.

3. **Wiring parties.** — No 1 wiring party (Sgt Stewart & 12 men) will complete and strengthen the existing wire between saps 1 and 2.

No 2 wiring party (Cpl. Johnson & 12 men) will complete and strengthen the existing wire between saps 2 and 3.

These two parties will be under Lt. P. Murray.

No 3 wiring party (Lt Curtin, Sgt Hyde & 20 men) will construct an entanglement between saps 3 and 4.

Material will be dumped for these parties as follows:—
    For No 1 party at the head of No 1 sap.
     "   " 2   "   "   "   "   " " 2 "
     "   " 3   "   "   "   "   " " 4 "

Gaps one yard wide will be left in the entanglement immediately at the South side of each sap head.

Working parties will commence work at 6 p.m.

Digging Parties.

4. **First Relief** — 3 Digging parties will be furnished by the 10th R. I. Rifles.

No 1 (4 Officers and 75 men) will march from Auchonvillers by the light railway to railhead in 2nd Avenue, thence by a track across country marked by a trail of chloride of lime to the front trench and so via No 2 sap to their task, which will be between No 1 & 2 saps, extending on it to the right. A guide will meet them at the 2nd Avenue Railhead.

No 2 (4 Officers and 75 men) will march via 2nd Avenue to No 3 sap and extend to the right on their task which will be from No 3 sap to No 2.

No 3 (2 officers and 125 men) will march via Old Beaumont Road to No 4 sap and extend to their right on their task which will be from No 4 sap to No 3.

The first relief will work from 6 p.m. to 12 midnight.
At 11:30 p.m. ~~midnight~~ each man of this relief will lay his tools down on his task and the parties will file away by their respective saps, turning to the right (North) into the fire trench on leaving the sap. When the last man is clear of the sap these parties will get on the fire step leaving the trench clear until the next relief have filed down the saps to their tasks.

2nd Relief.

2nd Relief will be of equal strength to the first relief.
The 3 parties will proceed by the routes detailed for the 1st relief and will be at their respective entrances to the fire trench by 12 midnight. They will not enter the fire trench until receiving word that the first relief is clear and on the firestep.
This relief will continue work until ordered to leave by O.C. 8th Bn. R. I. Rifles, when they will depart by the routes they came taking their tools with them.

5. Casualties. — Any casualties will be evacuated by the chloride of lime path or Old Beaumont Rd. to Auchonvillers.
A stretcher party will be in the fire trench near the mouth of each sap.

6. Bn Headquarters will be established at the Hd Qrs of the Right Company in 2nd Avenue, where all reports will be sent.

7. Communication. — Telephone communication will be established between Bn Hd Qrs (vide 6) and each sap head.

8. Dress. — Wiring and digging parties will wear one bandolier of ammunition and carry their rifles which will be loaded with 5 rounds before starting. No equipment or bayonets will be worn by these parties.

(Sgd) W. L. Campbell Lt. & Adjt.
8th Bn R. I. Rifles

107 Bde

8th Bn. Royal Irish Rifles.
War Diary

Instructions regarding War Diaries and Intelligence Summaries are contained in F. S. Regs., Part II. and the Staff Manual respectively. Title pages will be prepared in manuscript.

January 1917.

Army Form C. 2118.

WAR DIARY
or
INTELLIGENCE SUMMARY.
(Erase heading not required.)

Vol/4

Place	Date	Hour	Summary of Events and Information	Remarks and references to Appendices
In NEUVE EGLISE and SHANKILL HUTS.	1-1-17		Day observed as a holiday. Special dinner for the men.	
	2-1-17		Day devoted to parades and inspections. The London Gazette, 1st January '17. Capt. J. D. Nicholl and Capt. H. P. Thornton – Military Cross. Mentioned in Despatches. Capt. J. D. McCallum. D.S.O. 8/3162. Sgt. J. McKearnan and 8/3857. Sgt. S. Wilkinson.	
	3-1-17		The Battalion relieved the 15th Bn. Royal Irish Rifles. Good relief, complete at 5.30 p.m.	
In Trenches.	4-1-17		Quiet day; not much artillery activity.	
In Trenches.	5-1-17		Quiet day. Some orange flares observed to North of our sector.	
In Trenches.	6-1-17		Boshe shelled SURREY LANE and T.6.1, no damage.	
In Trenches.	7-1-17		Quiet day. Weather dull with rain.	
In Trenches.	8-1-17		Quiet day. Weather wet.	
In Trenches.	9-1-17		Relieved by the 15th Bn. Royal Irish Rifles. Good relief, complete at 5-4-5 p.m.	
In Billets at KORTEPYP CAMP.	10-1-17		Day spent in Kit, Rifle, S.A.A. and Clothing inspections. Weather, frosty.	

8th Bn. Royal Irish Rifles.   January 1917.   Army Form C. 2118.

WAR DIARY
or
INTELLIGENCE SUMMARY.
(Erase heading not required.)

Instructions regarding War Diaries and Intelligence Summaries are contained in F. S. Regs., Part II. and the Staff Manual respectively. Title pages will be prepared in manuscript.

Place	Date	Hour	Summary of Events and Information	Remarks and references to Appendices
In Billets.	11-1-17		Day devoted to baths.	
In Billets.	12-1-17		Found working parties for front and support lines.	
	13-1-17		Day spent in billets during which Company training was carried out. Found working parties.	
In Billets.	14-1-17		Company parades. In the afternoon we played the 9th Bn. Royal Irish Rifles in the 1st round of the "Withycombe Cup." We won 7-1.	
In Billets	15-1-17		We relieved the 15th Bn. Royal Irish Rifles, had a good relief, complete at 6.30 p.m.	
In Trenches.	16-1-17		Very quiet day. Heavy mist; threatening snow.	
In Trenches.	17-1-17		Snowing all night and intermittantly through day. Some hostile artillery activity in morning.	
In Trenches.	18-1-17		Quiet day. Some snow and rain.	
In Trenches.	19-1-17		Enemy artillery active in the morning, otherwise day quiet. Hard frost.	
In Trenches.	20-1-17		O.C. "C" Coy carried out a successful shoot with 18 pdr. Batty. Quiet day in our sector, still freezing.	

T2134. Wt. W708-776. 50C000. 4/15. Sir J. C. & B.

8th Bn. Royal Irish Rifles.   WAR DIARY   January 1917.   Army Form C. 2118.

Instructions regarding War Diaries and Intelligence Summaries are contained in F. S. Regs., Part II. and the Staff Manual respectively. Title pages will be prepared in manuscript.

INTELLIGENCE SUMMARY
(Erase heading not required.)

Place	Date	Hour	Summary of Events and Information	Remarks and references to Appendices
In Trenches.	21-1-17		Quiet day still freezing hard. Some artillery activity in morning and while relief was in progress. Relief began at 4.30 p.m., and complete at 6.35 p.m. Two companies 'C' & 'D' occupying FORBES TERRACE and FISHERS PLACE in reserve to 10th and 15th Bn. Royal Irish Rifles respectively, while A & B Companies moved to SHANKILL HUTS with Headquarters at NEUVE EGLISE as usual.	
In Billets.	22-1-17		Day occupied as usual after relief.	
In Billets.	23-1-17		Found working parties from all companies for Front and Support Lines. Heavy artillery strafe on our right, we "stood to" from 6-30 p.m. to 7.15 p.m. when dismissed.	
In Billets	24-1-17		Found working parties from all companies for Front and Support Lines. Companies changed over, A and B occupying FISHER'S PLACE and FORBES TERRACE respectively while C & D came to SHANKILL HUTS relief.	
In Billets.	25-1-17		Morning working party only. Day spent in preparing for relief.	
In Billets.	26-1-17		Battalion moved to METEREN area.	

Army Form C. 2118.

WAR DIARY
INTELLIGENCE SUMMARY
(Erase heading not required.)

8th Bn. Royal Irish Rifles.   January 1917.

Instructions regarding War Diaries and Intelligence Summaries are contained in F. S. Regs., Part II. and the Staff Manual respectively. Title pages will be prepared in manuscript.

Place	Date	Hour	Summary of Events and Information	Remarks and references to Appendices
	27-1-17		In Billets. Cleaning Billets, equipment, and inspection of rifles and gas helmets etc.	
	28-1-17		In Billets. Recreational Training carried out	
	29-1-17		In Billets. do.	
	30-1-17		In Billets. do.	
	31-1-17		In Billets. A and B. Coys Tactical Route March, C and D companies Recreational Training.	

Commdg. 8th Bn. Royal Irish Rifles.
Lt.Col.
HR Hamilton

8th Bn. Royal Irish Rifles.

WAR DIARY February 1917.

Army Form C. 2118.

INTELLIGENCE SUMMARY.
(Erase heading not required.)

Vol 15

Place	Date	Hour	Summary of Events and Information	Remarks and references to Appendices
On Service	1/2/17		Battalion in billets at METEREN. Section training carried out. Afternoon devoted to Recreational training	Lt Colonel Chitterwiler Commdg 8th Bn R.I. Rifles.
- do -	2/2/17		- do - - do -	
- do -	3/2/17		- do - - do -	
- do -	4/2/17		- do - - do -	
- do -	5/2/17		Battalion in billets at METEREN. Platoon training carried out. Afternoon devoted to Recreational training	
- do -	6/2/17		Battalion in billets at METEREN. Platoon training carried out. Afternoon - D. Coy played A Coy in Cole Hamilton League for 'Joint' Result :- D Coy 3 goals "A" Coy nil.	
- do -	7/2/17		Battalion in billets at METEREN. Platoon training carried out. Afternoon devoted to Recreational training.	
- do -	8/2/17		Battalion in billets at METEREN. Platoon training carried out. In the afternoon Battalion team played the 10th Bn Royal Ir. Rifles in the final of the WITHYCOMBE CUP. The 8th Bn Royal Irish Rifles winning by 4 goals to 1. After the match the cup was presented	

8th Bn. Royal Irish Rifles.

WAR DIARY
INTELLIGENCE SUMMARY

February 1917

Army Form C. 2118.

Place	Date	Hour	Summary of Events and Information	Remarks and references to Appendices
On Service	8.2.17		to the winners by the donor Brigadier General Wm. Withycombe, C.M.G., Comdg 107th Infantry Brigade, who congratulated the winning and losing teams, match was played at BAISIEUX.	Lieut Colonel Comdg 8th Bn R.I. Rifles.
-do-	9.2.17		Battalion in billets at METEREN. Platoon training carried out.	
-do-	10.2.17		Battalion moved to ALDERSHOT CAMP (T.19.b.7.9. Sheet 28 SW) being relieved by the 15th Bn Royal Irish Rifles	
-do-	11.2.17		Battalion in billets at ALDERSHOT CAMP. Platoon work carried out for 1½ hours, after that Divine Service. In the afternoon the final in the Brigade Bayonet Fighting on the training ground of the 25th Division at METEREN. Result:- 1st:- 107th M.G. Coy. 2nd - 8th & 9th Bn Roy. Ir. Rifles tie, 3rd - 15th Bn R.I. Rifles. 4th - 10th Bn Roy. Ir. Rifles.	
-do-	12.2.17		Battalion in billets at ALDERSHOT CAMP. Coy training carried out. In the afternoon in connection with Brigade Recreational programme D. Coy, Bal. Coy 8th R.I. Rifles played beat. boy, 9th R.I. Rifles at ALDERSHOT CAMP. Result: 8th Bn 4 goals. 9th Bn Nil.	

8th Bn. Royal Irish Rifles.

WAR DIARY

INTELLIGENCE SUMMARY.
(Erase heading not required.)

February, 1917

Army Form C. 2118.

Place	Date	Hour	Summary of Events and Information	Remarks and references to Appendices
On S'vances	13.2.17		Battalion in billets at ALDERSHOT CAMP. Coy training carried out. In the afternoon "D" Coy 8th R.I.Rifles played 107th M.G.Coy. in connection with Brigade Recreational programme. Result: 8th R.I.R. 5 goals. 107th M.G. Coy. 1 goal.	
-do-	14.2.17		Battalion in billets at ALDERSHOT CAMP. Coy training carried out. Afternoon - Recreation.	
-do-	15.2.17		Battalion in billets at ALDERSHOT CAMP. Coy training carried out. In the afternoon "D" Coy played Beal. Coy. 10th R.I.Rifles in connection with Brigade Recreational programme. Result: - "D" Coy 2. 10th R.I.R. nil	
-do-	16.2.17		Battalion in billets at ALDERSHOT CAMP. Coy training carried out. "D" Coy. inspected by Brig. Genl. 10 M.Withycombe, C.M.G. Comdg 107th Inf. Brigade in the Drill and turn out competition. Result:- 107th M.G.Coy. 1st, 10th & 15th R.I.Rifles tie 2nd, 8th Bn R.I.Rifles 3rd, 9th Bn R.I.Rifles 4th. In the afternoon "D" Coy played Beal. Coy 15th R.I.R. in connection with Brigade Recreational programme. Result:- "D" Coy. 4 goals. Beal. Coy. 15th R.I.Rifles nil. By winning this	

Pattensen Lt. Colonel
Comdg 8th Bn R.I Rifles.

WAR DIARY of 8th Bn. Royal Irish Rifles

Army Form C. 2118. February 1917.

Instructions regarding War Diaries and Intelligence Summaries are contained in F.S. Regs., Part II. and the Staff Manual respectively. Title pages will be prepared in manuscript.

INTELLIGENCE SUMMARY
(Erase heading not required.)

Place	Date	Hour	Summary of Events and Information	Remarks and references to Appendices
Bns Service Coy	16.2.17		Match "D" Coy, 8th Bn R.I. Rifles won the bal. boy in the Brigade. "D" Coy's record - played 4, won 4, goals for 15 against 1, points 8.	Allenmuller Lt. Colonel. Comdg 8th/Bn. R.I. Rifles.
do.	17.2.17		Battalion in billets at ALDERSHOT CAMP. Coy training carried out. Afternoon - Recreation.	
do.	18.2.17		Battalion marched to METEREN to take part in the cross country run for Brigade Recreational programme. Run was carried out by battalions, men who completed the course in 35 minutes to count. First 12 men of the Brigade home to receive medals, this Bn had 36 men finish in the time and winning 4 of the medals. Sgt J. Broft "D" Coy being the quickest man in the Brigade completing the course in 26 mins 37 secs, nearly 2 mins quicker than any man of the other Bns competing. Result of run - 107th M.G. Coy 1st, 8th R.I. Rif. 2nd, 9th R.I. Rif. 3rd, 15th R.I. Rif 4th, 10th R.I. Rif. 5th.	
do.	19.2.17		Battalion in billets at ALDERSHOT CAMP. Coy training carried out.	

8th Bn. Royal Irish Rifles.   WAR DIARY   February 1917.   Army Form C. 2118.

INTELLIGENCE SUMMARY.
(Erase heading not required.)

Place	Date	Hour	Summary of Events and Information	Remarks and references to Appendices
Ousourier	19.2.17		Afternoon - Recreation.	
do.	20.2.17		Bn. in billets at ALDERSHOT CAMP. Bn training carried out in the afternoon. 107th Bde Boxing competition carried out at the CAISSE D'EPARGNE, BAILLEUL. No 8/13202 Rfm J. McDONNELL winning the Middle-weight championship and medal, No 8/3118 Rfm J. Bingham losing on points in the final of the feather-weights.	
do.	21.2.17		Bn. in billets at ALDERSHOT CAMP. Bn training carried out. Afternoon - Coy inspections.	
do.	22.2.17		Bn. in billets at ALDERSHOT CAMP. Bn training carried out. Afternoon - Medical Inspection.	
do.	23.2.17		Bn. in billets at ALDERSHOT CAMP. Bn training carried out. Afternoon - Colo. Hamilton League completed, 'A' Coy v 'B' Coy. 'A' Coy winning by 5 to nil. 'B' Coy v 'D' Coy result - draw 1-1. winners of Colo. Hamilton Cup & medals - 'D' Coy. Record - played 6, won 4, drawn 1, lost 1, goals for 8, against, 3. points 9.	Lieut Colonel Commdg 8th Bn. R.I. Rifles.

8th Bn. Royal Irish Rifles.

WAR DIARY

INTELLIGENCE SUMMARY.

Army Form C. 2118.

February, 1917

Place	Date	Hour	Summary of Events and Information	Remarks and references to Appendices
On Service	24.2.17		Bn in billets at ALDERSHOT CAMP. Bn training carried out. In the afternoon Bn team played 9th Bn R. In. Fusiliers. Result:- 8th R.I. Rif. 5 goals, 9th Bn R. In. Fus. 4 goals.	(Roll Casualties:- Colonel Goode 8th Bn R.I. Rifles
-do-	25.2.17		Bn moved in to the DOUVE sector of trenches, relieving the 11th Bn Roy. Inniss. Fus., 109th Inft. Bde. A very good relief, completed by 5.50 p.m. 9th Bn R.I. Rifles on our left, 11th Bn R.I. Rifles on our right.	
-do-	26.2.17		In the trenches. A very quiet day.	
-do-	27.2.17		-do- Quiet day. Nothing of any importance.	
-do-	28.2.17		-do- -do-	

8th Bn Royal Irish Rifles

WAR DIARY

Army Form C. 2118.

March 1917

VOL/6

Place	Date	Hour	Summary of Events and Information	Remarks and references to Appendices
On Service	1-3-17		In the trenches. Quiet day. Weather fair.	
"	2-3-17		do. do. Quiet day. Weather fair.	
"	3-3-17		do. do. Relieved by the 15th Bn. R.S. Rifles in the line. Good relief. After relief the Battalion withdrew to billets in the Catacombs and was in Brigade Reserve.	
"	4-3-17		In Billets. Day devoted to Interior Economy.	
"	5-3-17		do. do. Battalion found working parties up to 250.	
"	6-3-17		do. do. do. do.	
"	7-3-17		do. do. do. do. 300.	
"	8-3-17		do. do. do. do. 300.	
"	9-3-17		do. do. Battalion went into the line and relieved the 15th Bn. R.S. Rifles. Good relief.	
"	10-3-17		In the Trenches. Fairly quiet day. Weather fair.	
"	11-3-17		do. do. Fairly quiet day. Weather fair.	
"	12-3-17		do. do. Relieved by the 3rd Bn. R.I.R. 108 Bde in the line. It very	
"	13-3-17		good relief. After relief the Batt. withdrew to Billets at the Catacombs	

8th Bn. Royal Irish Rifles.   March, 1917.

Army Form C. 2118.

WAR DIARY

(Erase heading not required.)

Instructions regarding War Diaries and Intelligence Summaries are contained in F. S. Regs., Part II. and the Staff Manual respectively. Title pages will be prepared in manuscript.

Place	Date	Hour	Summary of Events and Information	Remarks and references to Appendices
On Service	13-3-17		In Billets. The day was devoted to Interior Economy.	
"	14-3-17		The Battalion moved out and took over from the 47th 15de. 16th Division. This Battalion relieved the 6th Bn. The Royal Irish Regt. and Companies were situated as follows, Bn. Hqrs. DOCTORS HOUSE. N.21.7.6.6. - "A" Coy. COOKER FARM N.35.c.4.0.80. - "B" Coy. BEEHIVE Dug-outs N.34.B. - "C" Coy. FORT REGINA. N.28.A. - "D" Coy. LA POLKA. N.22. Central. (Reference Map Sheet. 28.S.W.) The Battalion moved by platoons at 4 minutes interval, Route HYDE PARK CORNER - PETIT PONT - X Roads LA TROMPE CABT - FORK Roads T.9.c. to DAYLIGHT CORNER at N.3.d.05.50. A very good relief completed about 6.30 p.m. Officers visited the New part of the line.	
"	15-3-17		The 15 Battalion in Brigade Support. Officers and N.C.O's visited New part of the line.	
"	16-3-17		The Batt. in Bde. Support. Officers and N.C.O's visited G.H.Q. Line.	
"	17-3-17		do. do.	
"	18-3-17		do. do. In the afternoon Regimental team played the 2nd Bn. The R.I. Regt. 16th Div. at DRANOUTRE. A very good game. Result - 0-0.	
"	19-3-17		In Brigade Support. In the evening the Battalion moved up to the new part of the line, with 2 Coys in the line, 1 Coy. Batt. Support & 1 Coy Batt. Reserve.	

Army Form C. 2118.

8th Bn. Royal Irish Rifles.   March, 1917.

WAR DIARY

(Erase heading not required.)

Place	Date	Hour	Summary of Events and Information	Remarks and references to Appendices
On Service	19-3-17		Battalion Sector from N.36.A.60.10. to N.30.C.52.50. Bn. Hqs at NEWPORT dugouts at N.30.A.60.50. The Sector known as SPANBROEK Sector.	
"	20-3-17		In the trenches. Quiet day.	
"	21-3-17		do. do. Quiet day.	
"	22-3-17		do. do. Quiet day.	
"	23-3-17		do. do. Quiet day.	
"	24-3-17		do. do. At 4 a.m. Enemy bombarded our line and attempted to raid, full report attached. The Divisional Commander asked the Commanding Officer to convey to all Officers, N.C.O.'s and Men of the Battalion especially those of the front line his warmest congratulations on their very fine performance, this was conveyed to the men by the Officers. The men greatly appreciated the Divisional Commander's kind words. — Remainder of day quiet.	
"	25-3-17		In the trenches. Quiet day. Battalion relieved in the line in the evening by the 15th Bn. R.I. Rifles. A fair relief, completed by 11.35 p.m. After relief Battalion withdrew to billets at DERRY huts at N.32.Central, and was in Brigade Reserve.	(Sd) A Macrory Lt.Col. Comdg 8th Bn Royal Irish Rifles

WAR DIARY

8th Bn. Royal Irish Rifles.

March 1917.

Army Form C. 2118.

Instructions regarding War Diaries and Intelligence Summaries are contained in F. S. Regs., Part II. and the Staff Manual respectively. Title pages will be prepared in manuscript.

(Erase heading not required.)

Place	Date	Hour	Summary of Events and Information	Remarks and references to Appendices
On Service	26.3.17		In Billets. The Divisional Baths at DRANOUTRE, allotted to the Battalion. Remainder of day devoted to Inspections etc.	
"	27.3.17		In Billets. The Battalion found working parties up to 250, on front line etc.	
"	28.3.17		do. do. do.	
"	29.3.17		do. do. do.	
"	30.3.17		do. do. do. Battalion Team played the 108th Field Ambulance in the afternoon & won by 5 to 2.	
"	31.3.17		In Billets. The Battalion moved up to the line in the Evening and relieved the 15th Bn. Royal Irish Rifles. It very good in self, finished by 11pm.	

H.H. Hamilton Lt Col
Comdg 8th Bn R I Rifles

8TH BN ROYAL IRISH RIFLES

Report of bombardment and attempted raid on our line.

The enemy's machine guns were much more active during the night. The activity was first noticed about midnight and was kept up till 3 a.m.

During the night the enemy put up a greater number of flares than is usual.

At 3.55 a.m. enemy machine guns opened, sweeping our parapet. At 4 a.m. the bombardment started, and at the same time two flares were sent up by our right company, and the enemy was noticed forming in his own wire; two more flares showed that a party of about 60 was heading towards our line. A heavy fire of rifles and lewis guns was brought to bear on this party, at the same time the S.O.S. was sent up, and the enemy turned and ran for his line, in disorder. Our lewis gun in the 'BULL RING' joined in with good effect on the enemy's flank. This fire was maintained in spite of the heavy fire and shrapnel which burst over our lines. Our artillery acted promptly and it thought that the raiding party was caught in our barrage.

The enemy put down a heavy artillery barrage, the left resting to the NORTH of LONG LANE, back to about 50 yards WEST of POND FARM, the whole front line, S.P.6, S.P.7, LONG LANE, REDAN AVENUE, ULSTER ROAD, KINGSWAY to COOKER FARM. The bombardment commenced at 4 a.m. with a salvoe of 77 mm shells which burst at S.P.6. The enemy sent over 5.9's, 4.2's, light, medium and heavy trench mortars, the greater number of which were directed against S.P.6. This was obviously the objective of the attempted raid.

The defences of S.P.6 were badly damaged. KINGSWAY was knocked in in seventeen places. ULSTER ROAD was broken in at the junction with LONG LANE. LONG LANE was broken in three places, the BULL RING and front line near the top of REDAN AVENUE receiving direct hits. In REDAN AVENUE there is a large crater about 25 feet deep and 30 feet wide which must have been caused by a very heavy minenwerfer. Direct hits were received on COOKER FARM and a dug-out close to COOKER FARM. The bombardment ceased about 5.25 a.m.

At 4.10 a.m. the platoons in the BULL RING were without communication. A 5.9 burst on the signallers dug-out cutting the wire and destroying the visual signalling lamp. It was quite impossible for runners to pass through the barrage on the right. However communication was kept up between left company and supports by means of runner, and with Bn.Hd.Qrs by wire. From early in the bombardment the right Company was cut off from Bn.Hd.Qrs. by wire or visual, communication was however eventually obtained by runners from Battalion Headquarters.

Various parts of the trenches were covered with pieces of flint (sample herewith). This apparently being what the enemy is using to fill his minenwerfers as no flint was noticed in the trenches previously.

At 4.5 a.m. a flare was sent up by the enemy which burst into 2 green stars, three more of these followed at five minutes interval.

Casualties - Killed   1 O.Rank
              Wounded   23   "

Lt-Col Hamilton Lt-Col
Comdg 8th Bn Royal Irish Rifles

24-3-17

N.B - Para 3, line 5 after "wire" insert "at about N.36.a.52.41.

8th Bn. Royal Irish Rifles.   April, 1917.   Army Form C. 2118.

WAR DIARY

Vol 17

Remarks: P.I.C. Hamilton Lt-Col. Comdg 8th Bn. Royal Irish Rifles.

Place	Date	Hour	Summary of Events and Information	Remarks and references to Appendices
On Service	1.4.17		In the trenches. Quiet day. Weather - bad.	
do.	2.4.17		do. do. Weather - bad.	
do.	3.4.17		do. do.	
do.	4.4.17		do. do.	
do.	5.4.17		do. do.	
do.	6.4.17		do. do.	
do.	7.4.17		do. Artillery activity otherwise quiet day. Weather - bad.	
do.	8.4.17		do. Relieved in the evening by the 1st Bn. R.I. Rifles. 109th Brigade. Good relief completed by 11.25 p.m.) After relief the Battalion, less Batt. Hqrs moved out to KEMMEL Hill and was in tents. Battalion Hd. Qrs. moved to Chateau at X.17.c.33. sheet 27 S.E.	
do.	9.4.17		In Camp. Day devoted to cleaning equipment etc.	
do.	10.4.17		do. do. Found working parties. 16 platoons of minimum strength 28 O.R. for work on Support Lines.	
do.	11.4.17		do. do. Found working parties. 16 platoons of minimum strength 28 O.R. for work on Support Lines.	

8th Bn. Royal Irish Rifles.   April. 1917.

Army Form C. 2118.

WAR DIARY

Place	Date	Hour	Summary of Events and Information	Remarks and references to Appendices
On Service	12.4.17		In Camp. Found working parties. 16 platoons of minimum strength 2 N.C.O's for work on Support Lines. Afternoon Battalion team played the E. Corps Siege Park and won easily 6-0.	
do.	13.4.17		In Camp. Found the same working parties. In the morning the Battalion Drums met and played the 2nd Bn. Royal Irish Regt through BAILLEUL for about 2 miles to STRAZEELE (16"Div") Very much appreciated by the Officers and Men of the 2nd Royal Irish Regt.	
do.	14.4.17		All work completed by 2 pm. Camp struck and Battalion marched to METEREN AREA.	
do.	15.4.17		Battalion marched to HAZEBROUCK AREA. An exceedingly good march.	
do.	16.4.17		Battalion marched to WIZERNES. B.G.C. 107 Bde. complimented the Battalion on excellent marching and march discipline.	
do.	17.4.17		Battalion marched to 2nd Army Training Area. Bn. Hd. Qrs and 3 Companies being billeted at ZOUDAUSQUES and one Company at MORLINGHEM.	
2nd Army Training Area.	18.4.17		Platoon Training commenced. Scouts & Signallers working as separate bodies.	
ZOUDAUSQUES	19.4.17		Platoon Training continued. Scouts & Signallers working as separate bodies.	

8th Bn. Royal Irish Rifles. April. 1917.

Army Form C. 2118.

WAR DIARY

(Erase heading not required.)

Instructions regarding War Diaries and Intelligence Summaries are contained in F. S. Regs., Part II. and the Staff Manual respectively. Title pages will be prepared in manuscript.

Place	Date	Hour	Summary of Events and Information	Remarks and references to Appendices
2nd Army Training Area	20-4-'17		Platoon training continued. Scouts and Signallers working as separate Bodies.	
ZOUDAUSQUES.	21-4-'17		Company training commenced. Scouts and Signallers working as separate Bodies	
"	22-4-'17		" continued. " do do do	
"	23-4-'17		" do " do do do	
"	24-4-'17		Battalion training commenced. Scouts & Signallers working with their Coys.	
"	25-4-'17		" continued. " do do do	
"	26-4-'17		" do " do do do	
"	27-4-'17		Brigade training commenced. Scouts & Signallers working with their Coys.	
"	28-4-'17		" continued. " do do do	
"	29-4-'17		Divine Service held. No other parades.	
"	30-4-'17		Bn. vacated Billets in ZOUDAUSQUES and marched to WIZERNES, via ETREHEM and WISQUES.	

J.L.H.Hamilton Lt. Col.
Comdg. 8th Bn. Royal Irish Rifles.

8th Bn. Royal Irish Rifles.

WAR DIARY

May. 1917.

Army Form C. 2118.

Vol 18

Place	Date	Hour	Summary of Events and Information	Remarks and references to Appendices
On Service	1-5-17		Battalion on line of march from Training Area ZUDAUSQUES near ST. OMER.	
"	2-5-17		Marched from HAZEBROUCK to METEREN. Battalion at METEREN in Divisional reserve. Day devoted to interior economy.	
"	3-5-17		Battalion at METEREN. Company parades were carried out. Battalion team played 107th Brigade and won 5-0.	
"	4-5-17		Battalion at METEREN. Company parades carried out.	
"	5-5-17		Battalion at METEREN. Company parades carried out. The Battalion 1st Line Transport moved to HOULLE by march route. The Battalion was awarded the following prizes at the 107th Inf. Bde. Horse Show held on 29-4-'17. Capt. J.M. REGAN. - 3rd Prize - jumping. Silver Matchbox. Capt. T.E. McKINNEY. - 3rd Prize. - Flat Race. Silver Matchbox. No. 3/12250. Rfm. J. DUNCAN. - 3rd Prize. - Best turnout. 1 pr. H.D. Horses in Limbered or L.S. Wagon. - 5.Frs. and No. 8/12450. Rfm. G. Walker. - 3rd Prize - Best turnout L.D. Horses in Limbered Wagon. - 5.Frs.	
"	6-5-17		Battalion entrained at HAAGEDORNE (BAILLEUL) and proceeded to HOULLE near St. OMER.	

Lt. Col. Cmndg 8th Bn. Royal Irish Rifles.

8th Bn. Royal Irish Rifles.   May 1917.   Army Form C. 2118.

WAR DIARY

Instructions regarding War Diaries and Intelligence Summaries are contained in F. S. Regs., Part II. and the Staff Manual respectively. Title pages will be prepared in manuscript.

Place	Date	Hour	Summary of Events and Information	Remarks and references to Appendices
On Service	7-5-17 to 11-5-17		Battalion at HOULLE. The Battalion carried out Musketry on 2nd Army Range; obtaining a very good report from Commandant, 2nd Army Musketry School. The following football matches were played:- Officers 8th Bn. R.I. Rifles v. Officers 21st London Regt.; result was 8th Bn. R.I. Rifles 2, 21st London Regt 1. The Battalion team played 21st London Regt. and the 26th Royal Fusiliers. Results. 8th Bn. R.I. Rifles 5, 21st London Regt 0 and 8th Bn. R.I. Rifles 8, 26th Royal Fusiliers 0.	Lt. Col. McCalmont 8th Bn Royal Irish Rifles.
"	12-5-17		Battalion entrained at WATTEN moving up to METEREN area.	
"	13-5-17		Battalion at METEREN. Divine Services held.	
"	14-5-17		Battalion moved to Reserve Bde. Area. S.4.D.7.3. Map Ref. 28.S.W. (near DRANOUTRE)	
"	15-5-17 to 25-5-17		Battalion found working parties, all available men except signallers, Scouts and Snipers who underwent special training under the Intelligence Officer, up to 25-5-17 when working parties up to 270 O.Rs. were discontinued.	
"	26-5-17		Battalion in Reserve Bde Area. Company & Battalion parades carried out.	do.
"	27-5-17		do.	do.

8th Bn. Royal Irish Rifles.

WAR DIARY

May, 1917.

Army Form C. 2118.

Instructions regarding War Diaries and Intelligence Summaries are contained in F.S. Regs., Part II. and the Staff Manual respectively. Title pages will be prepared in manuscript.

(Erase heading not required.)

Place	Date	Hour	Summary of Events and Information	Remarks and references to Appendices
On Service	28-5-17		Battalion in Reserve Bde. Area. Company & Battalion parades carried out.	
" "	29-5-17		do. do. do.	
" "	30-5-17		Battalion moved to the IX Corps Training Area at BERTHEN	
" "	31-5-17		Battalion at BERTHEN Area. Battalion practised attack over Dummy Trenches.	

A.C.B.Bowlder Lt-Col.
Comdg 8th Bn. Royal Irish Rifles.

8th Bn. Royal Irish Rifles.   Army Form C. 2118.

WAR DIARY

INTELLIGENCE SUMMARY

(Erase heading not required.)

June 1917.

107/36

Place	Date	Hour	Summary of Events and Information	Remarks and references to Appendices
	June '17			
BERTHEN Area	1st		Battalion practised attack over dummy trenches at R.11.c. (Ref sheet 27. S.E. 2nd Edit)	
"	2nd		"	
"	3rd		"	
"	4th		"	
"	5th		"	Orders for attack on 7th June 1917 attached.
From "	6th		Battalion moved to No 3 Concentration Area at DRANOUTRE where Bomber sand-bags	
To No 3 Area DRANOUTRE	6th		Rations, etc., were issued to all ranks. A hot meal was issued to the men at about 8 p.m.. At 9.30 p.m. the Battalion paraded (wee wiry hopply) and moved off by platoons at 2 minutes interval to the Assembly Trenches first behind the	
To Assembly Trenches.	7th		front line trenches at N.35.d. and N.36.6. (Ref WYTCHAETE. 28. S.W.2. Ed.5.A) where the remainder of Bombs, trench carriers, etc, were issued to all ranks. The men were remarkably cheery.)	
Blue Line	7th		At 3.10 a.m. attack started. See Narrative of Operations attached.	
Fort Victoria	8th		Orders received from 107th Infantry Brigade that the Battalion would be relieved off	
			The 12th Battalion Royal Irish Rifles relieved this Battalion in the Blue Line. See	
		9 a.m.		

2"Bn. Royal Irish Rifles.

Army Form C. 2118.

WAR DIARY
or
INTELLIGENCE SUMMARY.
(Erase heading not required.)

June 1917.

Place	Date	Hour	Summary of Events and Information	Remarks and references to Appendices
	June 17.			
Fort Victoria	8th		Narrative attached. Relief complete 10.30 a.m. After relief Battalion withdrew to bivouacs at FORT VICTORIA N.28.c. (Ref 28. SW.) Battalion all in at FORT VICTORIA at 1.15 p.m.	
	9th		Battalion relieved by Unit of 32nd Brigade. After relief Battalion withdrew to Bivouacs at No. 3 Concentration Area. On arrival in camp the Commanding Officer, Lt Colonel C.G. Cole-Hamilton, D.S.O. spoke to the Battalion and congratulated them on their very fine performance and excellent work during the attack of the 7th June 1917.	Moyer Battalion. Coming 8th for Royal Irish Rifles.
No. 3 Area.	10th		Battalion in bivouack. Day devoted to Interior Economy after Divine Service.	
"	11th	"	" " " Day devoted to Company parades and baths.	
"	12th	"	" " " The Battalion paraded 9.30 a.m. when the Brigadier Commanding 107th Infantry Brigade (Brigadier General W.M. Withycombe C.M.G.) addressed the Brigade on their brilliant performance on the offensive of 7th June 1917. The General Officer Commanding also read a letter of Congratulation from the General Officer Commanding 36th Division (Ulster). The Brigadier Commanding thanked the Brigade for their magnificent work.	

8th Bn. Royal Irish Rifles.

WAR DIARY
INTELLIGENCE SUMMARY
(Erase heading not required.)

June 1917

Army Form C. 2118.

Place	Date	Hour	Summary of Events and Information	Remarks and references to Appendices
No. 3 Area	June 13th		Battalion in bivouacs. Found working parties for forward area. 4 Officers 9 N.C.O's 280 Other Ranks. Remainder of Battalion Parade morning. Afternoon Battalion moved to No.13 Area in 6.18.2 A and Coppel and were in bivouacs.	Major [signature]
No.13 Area	14th		Battalion in bivouacs. Day devoted to Company Parades and baths.	
"	15th	"	"	
"	16th	"	"	
"	17th	"	Morning devoted to checking equipment etc. At 6 p.m. Battalion moved	
FORT VICTORIA	18th		to bivouacs at FORT VICTORIA.	
"	19th		During the morning Kit and Rifle inspection. In the evening the Battalion moved up to the trenches in O.27.B. (Ref. 28. S.W.) and relieved the 6th Bn Yorkshire Regt. Relief complete at 1.15 a.m. Very good relief.	
Trenches	20th		In the Trenches. Battalion Sector heavily shelled throughout day, but men were cheery. Casualties 1 died of wound. 6 wounded. (All other ranks)	
"	21st	"	Battalion Sector shelled. No effect on men. Casualties 8 O.Ranks killed 7 Other ranks wounded. 2 missing. 7 N.Y.D.N.	Forwarded 8th Bn Royal Irish Rifles

Army Form C. 2118.

WAR DIARY
INTELLIGENCE SUMMARY.
(Erase heading not required.)

8th Bn. Royal Irish Rifles.   June 1917.

Place	Date	Hour	Summary of Events and Information	Remarks and references to Appendices
Trenches	June 22nd		In the trenches. Battalion Sector shelled. No effect on men. Casualties 1 O.R. wounded.	
"	23rd		" " " " " 2 O.R. killed, 3 O.R. wounded.	
"	24		" " heavily shelled " " 4 O.R. wounded	
			Battalion relieved in the line by 15th Bn Royal Irish Rifles. Relief complete 1.15 a.m. Bad relief.	
			After relief Battalion withdrew to support line with Headquarters at LUMM FARM and were in Brigade Support.	
	25.		Battalion in Brigade Support. Quiet day, intermittent shelling, no casualties.	
	26.		" " " " " "	
	27.		" " " " " "	
			In the evening Battalion relieved in support trenches by 10th Royal Fusiliers, 111th Brigade. Relief complete 1 a.m. good relief. After relief Battalion withdrew to billets at DRANOUTRE. Arrived in billets 3 a.m. men very tired but very cheery.	Formed 8th Bn Royal Irish Rifles Major
	28.		Battalion in billets at DRANOUTRE. Day devoted to Interior Economy.	
	29.		Battalion marched to Billets at OUTTERSTEENE. Very good billets, arrived in billets 11. a.m.	
	30.		Battalion in billets at OUTTERSTEENE. Day devoted to Interior Economy and baths.	

OPERATION ORD RS NO 105
5th June 1917.

1. The Second Army will assume the offensive this month.
   The attack will take place on Zero day and will be preceded by several days bombardment.
   The attack will be made on the 36th Div Front with 2 Brigades in front and one in Divisional Reserve.
   The 107th Brigade will be on the right and the 109th Brigade on the left and the 108th Brigade in Divisional Reserve.

2. Objective - Red Line, Blue Line, Green Line, Black Line.
   The 8th & 9th Bns R.I.Rifles will attack the Red and Blue Lines the 10th & 15th Bns R.I.Rifles will ~~attack~~ pass through the 8th & 9th Battalions and attack the Green and Black Lines.

3. Boundaries - The Divisional, Brigade and Battalion Boundaries are shown by Yellow on M.O. Map issued to all concerned.

4. Company Objectices -
   Red Line :-
      B Coy on the right
      C " on the left
   Blue Line :-
      A Coy on the Right
      D " on the left

5. Formation of Attack - Each Company will attack in two waves of two lines each

6. Company Boundaries -
   Right Company to Red Line -
      Right Flank - German front line at N.36.b.00.15, thence by the stream in N.36.b. and O.31.a. to the Red Line at O.31.a.52.50.
      Left Flank - Junction of NATHAN LANE with German Front line at N.36.a.60.70 along NATHAN LANE to BONE POINT exclusive to O.25.c.50.00
   Left Company to Red Line -
      Right Flank - Junction of NATHAN LANE with German front line at N.36.a.60.70 along NATHAN LANE (exclusive) to BONE POINT inclusive to junction of OCCULT AVENUE and OCCULT TRENCH at O.25.c.50.00
      Left Flank - German front line at N.30.c.58.16, NARROW RESERVE at N.30.c.98.20 to Red Line at O.25.c.20.38, all exclusive.
   Right Company - Blue Line -
      Right Flank - Follow in rear of B Company to Red Line thence to OCCULT TRENCH at O.31.b.12.48, thence to Farm at O.31.b.75.82 thence along track and its prolongation at O.26.c.40.18, thence to Blue Line at O.26.c.78.38, inclusive.
      Left Flank - Red Line at O.25.c.55.00 to left edge of L'ENFER WOOD to Line at O.26.c.12.40, thence to Blue Line at O.26.c.50.70, all exclusive.
   Left Company - Blue Line - ~~Red Line~~
      Right Flank - Red Line at O.25.c.55.00 to left edge of L'ENFER WOOD to Line at O.26.c.12.40 thence to Blue Line O.26.c.50.70 all inclusive.
      Left Flank - Red Line at O.25.c.23.32 to line at O.25.d.80.70 thence to Blue line at O.26.c.10.78.

                                              continued -

- 2 -

7. <u>Directing flank</u> - The directing flank will be the Right, i.e. B Coy and then A Coy.

Guide for flank - along NATHAN DRIVE thence along track to the branch tracks at O.26.c.42.12, thence to Blue Line at O.26.c.78.35. Guide for latter reference - about 40 yards to the left from where the OCTOBER TRENCH touches the main road. O.C. B & A Coys will ensure that they have 1 N.C.O. and 4 reliable men on their flank to direct the advance.

8. <u>Position of Assembly</u> - Assembly trench map attached.

1st Wave, B Coy, i.e. 5 & 6 Platoons, from A to C, dividing line between platoons D/N/A B.

1st Wave, C Coy, i.e. 10 & 11 Platoons, from C to E, dividing line between platoons D.

2nd & 3rd Wave, i.e. 7 Platoons B Coy and 1 & 2 Platoons A Coy from F to H. Dividing line between platoons - 1 & 2 Platoons F to G, No 7 Platoon G to H.

2nd & 3rd Wave, i.e. 12 Platoon C Coy, 13 & 14 Platoons D Coy from H to K. Dividing line between platoons - 13 & 14 Platoons from H to I, No 12 Platoon C Coy from I to K.

4th Wave, i.e. No 3 Platoon A Coy from L to M, No 15 Platoon D Coy from N to O.

9. <u>Brigade and Battalions on our right flank</u> - The 7th Brigade will be on the right of the 8th Bn R.I.Rifles - Battalions on the Right of the 8th Bn R.I.Rifles -

    To first objective   -   8th Bn North Lancashires
    To second objective -   10th Bn Cheshire Regiment
    To third objective   -   1st Bn Wiltshire Regt.

10. <u>Artillery time table of lifts</u> - The Artillery barrage will advance by lifts of about 100 yards, and a map showing successive lifts is issued to Company Commanders herewith.

The leading waves will go over the parapet at Zero and the times of arrival and departure from the successive objectives are as follows :-

	Arrive	Depart
Red Line	0.35	0.50
Blue Line	1.40	3.40
Green Line	4.10	4.20x
Black Line	4.30	-

x - The Right of the 107th Brigade does not move.

11. <u>Nomenclature of days</u> - The first and successive days of bombardment will be known as V, W, X, Y & Z Days. Z Day will be the day of the assault.

12. <u>Infantry Attack</u> - The attack commences at Zero time on Z Day.
All movements on Z Day are timed from Zero.
Clock hour of Zero will be notified later.
<u>Right Coy to Red Line</u> - B Coy - B Coy will attack on the right from the German front line to Red Line (boundaries as on Page 1).

Possible obstacles - succession short trenches South of BONE POINT.

This Company must also be on the lookout to safeguard its flank in case the Company on its left is held up at BONE POINT.

In the event of the Left Company being checked at BONE POINT the advance must not be held up. The O.C. this Coy will also detail 1 N.C.O. and 4 men to be specially selected to Guide the Advance as detailed on page 1.

continued -

- 3 -

12. Infantry Attack - continued -

On arrival at Red Line one section from each Platoon having been previously detailed will Mop Up Red Line on its own platoon front working from Right to left both inclusive. On completion of Mopping Up the Company will be reorganized and will follow in support of the 3rd and 4th Waves, which will have passed through them.

On arrival at trench running from O.26.c.48.20 to O.25.d.80.70 one platoon of this company having been previously detailed will construct strong point 5, OCHRE END. This should be the No 3 Platoon or the third wave.

The left platoon will commence to consolidate this line by making a system of short trenches, these would be connected up later.

The right platoon (2 lines) will push on in support of A Coy attack on the Blue Line. This Platoon will not close up unless called upon by A Coy, but will lie up about 60 yards in rear of Blue Line.

Left Company to Red Line - C Coy - C Coy will attack on the left from the German Front Line to the Red Line (boundaries as on page 1)

Possible obstacles - Sunken Road in N.36.b. from N.36.b.22.88 to the Company Left Flank. BONE POINT - If a check is encountered at BONE POINT it will be attacked on its front by Rifle Grenadiers and Lewis Gun Fire, and on its flanks by Bombers and Riflemen, or as the circumstances at the time warrant.

On arrival at the Red Line one section from each platoon having been previously detailed will Mop up the Red Line on its own platoon front from Right to Left, until touch is obtained with 9th Bn R.I.Rifles On completion of mopping up the company will be reorganized and will follow in support of the 3rd and 4th Waves which will have passed through them.

On arrival at trench running from O.26.c.48.20 to O.25.d.80.70 two platoons, left and right platoons, will push on in support of D Coy's attack on the Blue Line. These platoons will not close up unless called upon by D Coy, but will lie up about 60 yards in rear of Blue Line.

1 Platoon, 2nd Wave will commence to consolidate this line by making a series of short trenches. These would be connected up later.

Right Company to Blue Line - A Coy - A Coy will attack on the Right from the Red Line to the Blue Line (boundaries as on page 1).

Possible obstacles - STEENEBEEK - L'ENFER WOOD - possible wire in L'ENFER WOOD - Dugouts in East end of L'ENFER WOOD - Trench running from O.26.c.50.20 to O.25.d.80.70.

If difficulty is encountered at L'ENFER WOOD it should be attacked on the front by Rifle Grenadiers and Lewis Gun Fire and on the Right by Bombers and Riflemen of A Coy, and by the First Line of the Right Wave of D Coy on the left flank assisted by Stokes Mortars which would be brought up as close as possible to a position to be selected by the O.C. Gun.

On arrival at trench O.26.c.50.20 to O.25.d.80.70, the last line of the rear wave having been previously detailed will mop up the trench from Company Right Flank to Company Left Flank until touch is obtained with Company on left. The other waves having passed through to the Blue Line. On completion of mopping up this line the wave will rejoin its platoon.

As the barrage will rest on the actual Blue Line for 2 hours, it will be practically impossible for Companies to occupy the whole of the Blue Line and the following procedure will be adopted - Companies will push up as close to the barrage as possible and will dig in on this line. When the barrage lifts the O.C. Coy will decide whether he will occupy the Blue Line as detailed or stop in the line he has started to dig.

continued -

12. **Infantry Attack - continued -**

Left Company to Blue Line - D Coy - D Coy will attack on the left from the Red Line to the Blue Line (boundaries as on Page 1).

Possible obstacles - STEENEBEEK - EARL FARM - System of trenches at O.25.d.98.52 - Trench running from O.26.c.50.20 to O.25.d.80.70. It is possible that the right company may meet with difficulty at L'ENFER WOOD. If this happens the front line of the leading wave on the right having been preiously detailed will attack the wood on the left flank with Lewis Gun Fire and Bombs. This must be carefully explained to the men as as little time as possible should be lost in the attack on the flank.

On arrival at trench O.26.c.50.20 to O.25.d.80.70, the last line of the rear wave having been previously detailed will mop up this trench working from Coy Right Flank to Coy Left Flank until touch is obtained with 9th Bn R.I.Rifles on the Left Flank. The other waves having passed through to the Blue Line.

On completion of Mopping Up this line this wave will rejoin its platoon.

As the barrage will rest on the actual Blue Line for 2 hours it will be practically impossible for companies to occupy the whole of the Blue Line as detailed and the following procedure will be adopted - Companies will push up as close to the barrage as possible and will dig in in this line. When the barrage lifts the O.C. Coy will decide whether he will occupy the Blue Line as detailed or stop on the line he has started to dig

Distance between Waves and Lines - It is essential that all the assaulting troops should be into 'NO MANS LAND' as quickly as possible without getting mixed up. When in 'NO MANS LAND' waves and lines will open out to the following -

30 yards between lines and 100 yards between waves.

O.C. A & D Coys are reminded that B & C Coys, although allotted special tasks after the capture of the Red Line are in support to the attack on the Blue Line and if the necessity arises should be called upon to throw weight where the fight may be going bad.

L'ENFER WOOD - As the wood will probably receive special attention from the enemy's artillery it must be impressed on all ranks the great necessity of keeping up as close to our barrage as possible, also of moving forward immediately the barrage lifts. This will undoubtedly lessen casualties and make the capture of the objectives a more simple matter.

The 8th Battalion on the Blue Line must be prepared to reinforce the 15th Bn R.I.Rifles in their attack on the Black Line if required.

If it is seen that the 15th Bn R.I.Rifles require assistance O.C. B & C Coys will immediately move up their Companies to reinforce the 15th Bn R.I.Rifles. All concerned are reminded that the Battalion is responsible for the consolidation and defence of the Blue Line and no matter what happens must not retire from that defence. For that reason A & D Coys will not move forward from the Blue Line no matter what happens. For this reason A & D Coys are held responsible for the consolidation and defence of the Blue Line.

13. **Moppers up -** I Company of 12th Bn R.I.Rifles will act as Moppers Up for area up to the Red Line exclusive and will follow in rear of the leading waves of B & C Coys.

One company of the 12th R.I.Rifles will mop up the area exclusive between the Red Line and the Blue Line, and will follow in rear of the 3rd Wave.

continued -

- 5 -

14. **Consolidation** - The responsibility for the consolidation is as follows :-

      Red Line - 12th Bn R.I.Rifles
      Blue Line - A & D Coys, 8th Bn R.I.Rifles

Each objective after capture will be consolidated and strong point established. All stores such as wire etc found round the enemy's line will be used for the construction of the strong point and consolidation as far as possible

15. **Medical** - Orders re Medical arrangements have been issued to Medical Officer.
    Regimental Aid Post - No 4, between S.P.6 and S.P.7 on the STRAND.

16. **Communication Trenches** - The following communication trenches will be used by this Battalion :-
    GEORGE STREET will be used as UP trench.
    KINGSWAY   " " " " DOWN "

17. **Battalion Headquarters** - Battalion Headquarters will be established at S.P.6, KINGSWAY.

18. **Equipment** - Dress - Battle order. Water proof sheets with cardigan rolled inside will be strapped to the back of the belt. The roll to be the length of the pack.

Each man will carry two sandbags worn on the belt in the manner shown to O.C. Companies.

In the haversack will be carried shaving and washing kit, one pair socks, iron rations and rations for Z Day.

Wire cutters will be carried by the leading waves of each platoon.

Distinguishing flags will be carried by one man per section but will only be unfurled by the most advanced troops.

    <u>Riflemen Section</u> - Haversack on back.
        2 Bombs for every man in side pockets.
        2 Sandbags per man.
        170 Rounds S.A.A.

    <u>Bombers Section</u> - Haversacks on backs.
        Throwers : 6 Mills Bombs carried in Canvas bag slung on belt
        Bayonet Men : 2 Mills Bombs in side pockets
        Remainder : 14 Mills Bombs in Canvas Buckets
        Every man : 120 rounds S.A.A. and 2 Sandbags

    <u>Rifle Bombers Section</u> - Haversacks on back or side in accordance with manner in which Grenade Carrier is used.
        Every man : Wooden Grenade Carrier holding 10 grenades
                  cartridges in pockets
             : 2 Mills Bombs in pockets
             : 120 rounds S.A.A.
             : 2 Sandbags

    <u>Lewis Gun Section</u> -
        No 1. Haversack at Side, carries gun in Special Lewis Gun carrier slung on YUKON PACK principle
        No 2. Haversack at side, spare parts, 4 magazines in Lewis Gun Magazine Carriers slung across shoulder.

Remaining 5 men - 6 magazines apiece in Lewis Gun Carrier slung across shoulder. Haversacks on back.

Every man 2 Mills Bombs, 120 rounds S.A.A. & 2 sandbags.

The remaining magazines will be kept at Battalion Dumps and will be sent up as required.

                                          continued -

18. **Equipment - continued -**

   Scouts - Scouts will carry haversack, rifle and 1 bandolier S.A.A..

   Intelligence Sections will wear the green distinguishing band on the left sleeve of the tunic at the wrist, the Battalion Sections with it sewn on straight round, the Brigade Section sewn on chevron-wise -

19. **Contact Aeroplanes** - Green flares will be carried by officers and reliable N.C.O's and men. These flares only to be lit when called for by the aeroplane and should be lit <u>only</u> by the most advanced troops.

   Flares to be lit either in the bottom of the trench or in shell holes - shell holes for preference.

   2 Flares per man will be carried.

20. **Maps** - All Officers will carry 1/10,000 28 S.W.2 WYTSCHAETE Map. This map will be referred to in all messages and reports. Maps of our trenches are not to be carried.

   No Officer, N.C.O. or man will carry any map showing any part of our present line. This part should be cut off the issued map and destroyed.

21. **Information** - It must be impressed upon all the importance of sending back every bit of information available, not only of our own doings but also the progress of the unit on our flanks. Negative information is also of the greatest value.

   No document or papers that would be of use to the enemy's will be carried.

22. **Carrying Party** - 2nd Lt English and the 4 N.C.O's and 46 O.Ranks already detailed will march up with the Battalion and when at GEORGE STREET will break off from the Battalion and will assemble in the STRAND.

   8th Bn R.I.Rifles on the right.

   As soon as the men are in position 2nd Lt English will report to Lieut Haig at REGENT DUGOUTS.

   An additional party of Sgt Boyle, 11 Drummers and 8 men to be detailed by Companies will form the Brigade Carrying Party. This party will proceed with the above party and will be under the direct orders of 2nd Lt English until arrival at Brigade. 2nd Lt English will report for both parties to Lieut Haig. The 15 YUKON PACKS will be carried up by this party.

   To make the second party up to 20 O.C. Coys will detail the following to report to 2nd Lt English on arrival in Camp to-morrow.

   A Coy - 2 O.R.   B Coy - 2 O.R.   C Coy - 2 O.R.   D Coy - 2 O.R.

   Equipment - Rifle, sword, entrenching tool, haversack at side, no bombs, 120 rounds S.A.A.

23. **Stretcher Bearers** - All stretcher bearers will proceed to the assembly trenches with their Companies, and will remain with them to evacuate casualties until Zero hour when they will proceed to the R.A.P. and report to M.O.

24. All forward messages will be sent direct to Brigade who will forward messages to Battalion Headquarters.

25. **Fixing of Swords** - Swords will not be fixed until 5 minutes before Zero.

continued -

26. **Lewis Guns** - The surplus Lewis Guns and teams of B & C Coys, i.e. their 4th Gun and team will remain at S.P.6 as Battalion Reserve.

27. **Telescopic Sights** - 50% of Telescopic Sights to be handed in to Quartermaster.

28. **Rum** - Any issue of rum will be made at a time as near Zero as possible.
  2 Bottles of Rum will be issued to each Platoon Commander and O.C. Detachment to-morrow.

29. **Officers Dress** - All Officers will be dressed and equipped the same as the men. Badges of rank will be worn on the shoulder strap.

30. **Tanks** - Two tanks have been allotted to this Brigade to assist in the attack from the Blue to the Black Line. It must be impressed upon every man that the tanks are there to assist this advance if possible, but he must never suppose that success depends on their presence. The men must never wait for the tank but must push on to their objective irrespective of whether they come up or not. There is a great danger of the attack being held up if this is not thoroughly realised by all ranks.

31. **Signal Communication** The party forming the Brigade Forward Station will follow immediately in rear of the last wave of the 8th and 9th Bn R.I.Rifles and establish themselves as quickly as possible on SPANBROEKMOLEN.
  The Battalion forward parties of the 8th & 9th R.I.Rifles will commence to move forward at ~~/~~/~~/~~/~~/~~/~~/~~/~~/~~ Zero plus 1.40.

32. **Requirements after Zero** - The Transport Officer and Quartermaster are held responsible that S.A.A., Bombs, Water and rations are made up in suitable loads ready to be sent forward immediately the request for same is received.
  When the use of pack animals is possible request for S.A.A. and supplies for the fighting line will be forwarded by Cyclist Orderly to the transport lines of the unit.
  The Quartermaster or his representative will be responsible that the ammunition or supplies asked for are despatched without delay, and will give the cyclist orderly an acknowledgement of the demand.
  R.E. Stores required by Battalions will be sent up in a similar manner, but in this case the pack animals will be loaded up with the required stores at N.29.a.1.1., N.35.a.7.8., N.29.c.3.5. or at DAYLIGHT CORNER or LINDENHOEK as may be most convenient.
  To provide the number which will be required by him each Battalion will send 1 driver and 1 pack animal with saddles but without crates to 122nd Field Coy R.E. at N.26.a.2.1. to report to O.C. that Company at 8 a.m. on Zero Day.

33.- **Dumps** - The dump at S.P.6 is allotted to this Battalion.

34. **Very Light Pistols** - 2 Very Light Pistols will be carried by the C.S.M. of each Company.

continued -

35. **Hectograph Message Forms and Maps** - 150 Hectograph Message Forms and report forms combined have been received and are issued herewith as follows :-

        A Company - 25
        B   "   - 25
        C   "   - 25
        D   "   - 25
        Intelligence Officer - 20
        Signalling Officer - 20
        Battn. Hd. Qrs - 10

These should be kept as far as possible by the people who would actually be sending back messages.. It is not necessary for the sender to strike out all of the ten subheads which he is not using.

It will save time if a cross (X) is put against the subheading to which attention is called.

On some of the Hectograph Maps it is noticed that EARL FARM (O.35.d.3.5.) has been marked as SCOTT FARM. This should be changed where necessary.

36. **Bombs** - The two bombs per man will be issued to-morrow at the Camp, also iron rations and the two sandbags.

The additional bombs will be issued when in the assembly trenches.

37. **Move to Assembly Trenches** - In order to bring attacking troops into their assembly trenches on Y/Z Night moves will take place in accordance with the following :-

Red Lamps will be placed along tracks A & B.
This Battalion will use track A.
So as to make movement easy guides will be at Camp on Y/Z night to conduct platoons to their assembly trenches. One guide per platoon.

On arrival at assembly trenches all troops must keep clear of the tracks and Communication trenches, so that troops in rear are not delayed nor communication hampered.

The assembly must be carried out silently. All bayonets to be dulled.

On arrival in Camp to-morrow each O.C. Coy will cause two men per platoon to parade two hours after arrival in camp to proceed to Battalion Dump at S.P.6 and collect the required number of Lewis Gun Drums, Bombs and Rifle Bombs from the above dump and make Platoon dumps of them on a convenient spot as near as possible to that portion of trench detailed for the platoon. 1 Officer per Company will proceed with this party. He should know the requirements of each article for his platoon.

The assembly of the Battalion to be completed by 2.30 a.m. by which hour all stores must have been issued.

The completion of assembly to be reported to Bn.Hd.Qrs, S.P.6 by the Code Word 'FACT'.

The Battalion will parade on Y/Z night in the Camp field to proceed to the assembly trenches as follows :-

        A Company - 9.35 p.m.
        B   "   - 9.40 p.m.
        C   "   - 9.45 p.m.
        D   "   - 9.50 p.m.
        Bn.Hd.Qrs - 9.55 p.m.

Platoons will move at 100 yards interval and will move off at above stated hours.

continued -

38. **Mines** - Mines opposite the Brigade Front will be exploded at Zero hour. If the explosion has not taken place by 15 seconds after Zero it is to be understood that it will not take place at all.

39. **S.O.S.Signal** - The S.O.S.Signall remain as at present, i.e. a single Red Very Light.

40. **Synchronising of Watches** - Capt J.M.Regan will report at 7 p.m. on Y/Z night at Brigade Headquarters at S.5.d.80.40 to obtain correct time.
He will again report at Brigade Headquarters in REGENT STREET Dugouts at 12 m.n. Y/Z night to synchronise watches again.

       Sgd. A.J.P.THORNTON, Captain & Adjt
         8th Bn R.I.Rifles

ADDENDUM

Page 7, Para 32, Requirements after Zero -
Immediately after this para please insert :-
'Petrol Tins are issued by the Divisional Train to Units as stated hereunder :-

For Water Carts.
 Each Infantry Battalion   100 tins) already issued
 Each M.G.Coy including T.M.Bty 50 tins)

For Pack Mules -
 Each Infantry Battalion   80 Tins) ~~already issued~~
 Each M.G.Coy including T.M.Bty 20 tins)

The vital necessity of bringing back petrol tins sent forward to the troops should be impressed on all ranks. The available supply of tins is very limited and there would be great difficulty in making up large deficiencies at short notice.
It may be assumed that units in front will be almost entirely dependent on petrol tins for their water supply for two or three days after Zero.

       Sgd. A.J.P.THORNTON, Capt & Adjt
         8th Bn R.I.Rifles

S E C R E T   SECRET ORDER   Copy No 38

                                 6th June 1917

 To-day is Y Day, and the Battalion will move to the Assembly trenches to-night as per Operation Order No 105 d/- 5th June 1917, para 37.

 2nd Lt Henderson is held responsible that guides are with the respective platoons that they are guides for by 9.30 p.m. These guides should report to the O.C. Coys by that hour.

 The men of 2nd Lt Henderson's party who are to go over with the Battalion to-morrow will report to 2nd Lt Cochrane at S.P.6 on completion of their task.

 The men who are left out as part of 33% Reserve will be marched back to the Transport Lines by 2nd Lt Henderson.

 <u>Stretcher Bearers</u> - The number of Stretcher Bearers has been increased to 32. Each Company will now have 8 Stretcher bearers and not 4 as previously.

 These 8 men per Company should report to the Medical Officer as ordered by him.

        Sgd. A.J.P.THORNTON, Capt & Adjt
          8th Bn Royal Irish Rifles

CONTACT PATROLS.   APPENDIX "H"

1.   Aeroplanes for contact patrols will be R.E. 8 type and will be specially marked by a black flap attached to the rear of each lower plane. Photographs are being issued.

2.   Two contact aeroplanes will be in the air at the same time. One watching the area South of WYTCHAETE and the other WYTSCHAETE and the area North of the village.

Contact patrols will fly over the line and call for flares at the following hours, and any hours subsequent to those hours which special aeroplanes may be ordered. Troops will also be prepared to put out flares at any other time if the aeroplane calls for them :-

Zero plus 0.45.
Zero plus 2 hours.
Zero plus 4.20.
Zero plus 5.20.
Zero plus 6.30.
Zero plus 11 hours.

3.   Aeroplanes will call for flares and WATSON Fans by sounding a Klaxon horn and firing a "VERY" White Light.

4.   Green flares will be used. They should be lit in bunches of three each about 30 yards apart.
WATSON Fans will be used in conjunction with flares. The fans should be turn over every 2 seconds and not quicker, that is, the white side will be exposed to the aeroplane for two seconds and the dark side for two seconds, and so on. An issue of 25 fans per Battalion will be made as they become available.

5.   In order to obtain as early intimation as possible from our own aeroplanes of hostile counter-attacks, the following procedure will be adopted:-
On the hostile Infantry being seen to quit their trenches and advance, the observer will send down by wireless "S.O.S." followed by the Zone Call - no map co-ordinates will be given. This will constitute a request to our artillery to put up a barrage on their "S.O.S." lines in that particular zone.
In order to avoid unjustified calls R.F.C. Observers will be given to understand clearly that the "S.O.S." Signal is only to be used when Hostile Infantry have left their front trenches and are advancing in the open in the direction of our own lines.
A machine for the purpose will be up from Zero.

6.   R.F.C. Observers will be warned not to attempt to fire at or to drop bombs on the enemy, but will confine their reconnaissances entirely to observation and transmission of information.

7.   No aeroplane will be in the air before Zero.

8.   A schedule of Code Calls for aeroplanes to be sued by Divisions is attached.

CODE LETTERS FOR LIAISON BETWEEN INFANTRY & AIRCRAFT.

Division	Infantry Brigade	Code Letters.
36th	107th	L.D.
	108th	L.E.
	109th	L.F.

The addition of W, X, Y or Z to the Brigade Code letter will give the particular Battalion of the Brigade, according to the "Order of Battle".

SUMMARY of Offensive Operations on 7th
June, 1917 by 8th Battalion Royal Irish Rifles.

6th June 1917.

9.30 p.m.   Marched from DRANOUTRE Concentration Area to Assembly Trenches in Right Sub-sector.

7th June 1917.

2.35 a.m.   All companies in position in Assembly Trenches ready to push off.

3.10 a.m.   Mines exploded and Battalion left the trenches, B. Coy on the Right, C Coy on the left, followed respectively by A & D Coys. Owing to the craters formed by the mines direction was somewhat lost.

3.16 a.m.   Enemy putdown barrage on STRAND and our front line trench. At no time was this very heavy. The whole Battalion was well into "NO MAN'S LAND" before the barrage was put down. One machine gun was firing across our front from the right but it was quickly put out of action by the Division on our right.

3.45 a.m.   Reached RED LINE without encountering any serious opposition. Here we met a few small isolated parties of enemy who were dealt with, 30 to 35 prisoners were captured and sentnback.
    In this line there was a great deal ofmconfusion All units of first and second waves of attack, being mixed up with us.- 9th R.I.Rifles and several units of 25th Division. Wgen 12th Bn R.I. Rifles arrived they found some men of the 10th Cheshires consolidating the position/our front. The units were only partially sorted out when A & D Coys passed through the line. The Division on our right had started off by losing direction towards their right and so had created a large gap part of which they afterwards filled by turning almost a left turn which brought their men through our left flank.

4.7 a.m.   A & D Coys moved through the RED LINE D Coy encountered a large dug-out with a machine gun which was quickly overcome and 22 prisoners captured. The wire in front of the STEENBEEK was foundnto be only cut in a few places and temporarily stopped the attack. No.8/12519 L/Cpl J.A.Amour rushed forward into our barrage and under hostile machine gun fire and cut a passage through the wire. A Company captured three machine guns in the west side of L'ENFER WOOD. Another machine gun and crew was captured at EARL FARM. One machine gun was captured along with about 25 prisoners at about point C.25.d.1.1. A Company encountered considerable resistance on the South side of L'ENFER WOOD from well hidden machine guns. 2nd Lt. D.A.Moyles directed an attack on these with great skill and daring, and although severely wonded himself his party captured two machine guns and about 20 prisoners.

                                                       continued.

SPECIAL ORDER

by

MAJOR-GENERAL O.S.W. NUGENT, C.B., D.S.O.

COMMANDING

36th (ULSTER) DIVISION.

6th July 1917.

The Divisional Commander has much pleasure in publishing the following letter which he has received from IXth Corps :-

The following letter has been received from the Army Commander :-

To Lieut-General A. HAMILTON GORDON, C.B.

Commanding IXth Corps.

Orders have been received for the transfer of the 36th Division from your Corps and from the Second Army.

Before the Division's departure I should be glad if you will convey to them my regret that they are leaving us.

The Division showed a fine tenacity and determination during a long period when they were on the defensive; they trained and prepared themselves for the offensive with admirable thoroughness, and they carried out the attack on the 7th June with a dash and gallantry which made success certain.

The Division has rendered valuable services with the Second Army.

Sgd. HERBERT PLUMER, General.

Commanding Second Army.

In communicating the above message from the G.O.C. Second Army, the Corps Commander wishes to associate himself with this expression of regret at losing the 36th Division and admiration of the sterling qualities exhibited by the Division.

Sgd. J. PERCY, Brig-General.

19th June 1917.   General Staff, IXth Corps.

Sgd. L.J. COMYN, Lt-Colonel.
A. A. & Q. M. G.
36th Division.

7th June 1917.

4.50 a.m.   Reached second objective, BLUE LINE, and proceeded to consolidate. One machine gun and two large trench mortars and one light Granatenwerfer were captured in East side of ENFER WOOD. Just before reaching the objective A Company came under trench mortar fire from ENFER WOOD but did not suffer many casualties owing to their erratic fire. The position was at once consolidated and a trench dug. A strong point was made at O.25.d.90 85 for a garrison of 3 Lewis Guns, 2 Bombing sections, 25 Riflemen and 2 Vickers Guns belonging to the 25th Division, who had become separated from their units.

     There was found to be some of the 10th Cheshires mixed up with our men and on our right a gap between us and the 25th Division. A Company moved to their right to correct the interval, and B Company came up and filled the gap thus made. Touch was then obtainable with the 1st Wiltshires on our right.

7.30 a.m.   15th Bn Royal Irish Rifles passed through our line to attack the GREEN LINE.
     Consolidation of BLUE LINE continued.

8.40 a.m.   I went up to BLUE LINE to see how matters stood.

     I found there men of three Divisions all mixed up with my men. I sorted them out as well as I could and got them consolidating the BLUE LINE and S.P.6 ENFER POINT. There were parties of all units wandering about on my flanks, apparently lost and not knowing where they were. I was unable to find out any information about the position on the GREEN LINE but there appeared to be some confusion. Bombs and ammunition required. I then returned to Battalion Headquarters at S.P.6.

     During the morning ENFER WOOD was shelled, together with the surrounding ground by the enemy.

12.41 p.m.   Received information from U L E that U B A would occupy and consolidate the MAUVE LINE from C.27.d.29 to O.27.d.70.55.

1.30 p.m.   Received orders to advance my Battalion Headquarters.

2.50 p.m.   12th Bn Royal Irish Rifles passed through our line.

3.10 p.m.   Brigade of 11th Division attacked the OOSTAVERNE LINE. As far as we saw the attack was successful.

3.40 p.m.   Established Battalion Headquarters at O.31.b.30.3 Found Companies quite comfortable in line. Area behind line and particularly ENFER WOOD being shelled. Everything quite all right.

4.45 p.m.   Pack Mules under Lieut Battershill came up with water, S.A.A. and bombs.
     Work of consolidation continued. Men tired but with tails right up.

continued -

7th June 1917.

1.15 a.m.	Received orders from U L E that the Battalion will be relieved by the 12th R.I.Rifles and would on relief proceed to FORT VICTORIA. During the night the situation was normal. Enemy still continued to shell ENFER WOOD but we had few casualties.
9 a.m.	Battalion relieved by 12th Bn R.I.Rifles.
10.30 a.m.	Relief complete.
1.15 p.m.	All the Battalion back in FORT VICTORIA.

REMARKS.

The Artillery barrage was too fast on account of the ground being so badly cut up. This especially applies to the Left Company as they had to go round the craters formed by the mine explosions

The system of communication was not a success. Telephone communication was very intermittent owing to wire being cut by shelling., and no attention was apparently paid to attempts to establish connection by visual with Divisional O.P. etc.

Artillery preparation was very good.

Many units showed complete lack of knowledge of where they actually were on the ground and lost direction frequently. On the Battalion front alone there were representatives of practically every unit in 16th, 36th and 25th Divisions. Greater care should be taken to acquaint all Officers at least with the ground over which they have to attack.

Loads for men carrying Lewis Gun Magazines are too heavy considering the ground they had to travel over on 7th inst.

Moppers up should follow attacking wave more closely so as to ensure that the enemy cannot come out of dug-outs after attack has gone on and shoot the attacking troops in the back.

A section of 1 N.C.O. and 4 men on directing flank of right company was found a great success. Their job was simply to keep direction. The left company lost direction somewhat owing to men of other units getting mixed up with them. There was a gap between our left and the 9th Bn R.I.Rifles in the BLUE LINE which was afterwards corrected. This was caused, it is supposed, by men of various units having originally filled this gap and having afterwards withdrawn.

Re Communications. 1 Officer, 1 Sergt, 2 Cpls and 10 O.Ranks, all specially trained and lightly equipped, should go forward after the attacking waves Their sole job would be to collect and send back information of the situation both of their own troops and of the troops on either flank. This party would be quite distinct from the ordinary intelligence party of the Battalion who have so many various duties to perform that they cannot be counted on to send back information.

continued -

The importance of early information is so great that I consider that this duty should be performed by a special party and not depend on signal communication and officers in the fighting line who have their hands full.

Rallying Flag. I would suggest in future a rallying flag should be carried by each company to enable men who have become separated through any cause to locate and rejoin their Companies.

Lewis Gun Carriers. Reports on the utility of the Lewis Gun carrier vary. It would appear that with short men the gun in the carrier bumps up and done and strikes the calves of the legs and the back of the head.

With the carrier more time is taken to get the gun into action, and frequently the string of the carrier gives trouble and has to be broken.

Yukon Packs. The Yukon Pack is a great advantage to carrying parties, as not only can a man carry up to 100 lbs without much effort but he has the use of both hands when going over badly broken ground. It is considered that the pack should be reduced in width by about 3 inches, as with all loads tried it was found that there was margin of about 3 inches over. A tight binder at top and bottom always held the load securely, and only in a very few cases was trouble experienced with the load working loose.

Pack Animals, loads for. The best way to carry barbed wire on pack animals is in biscuit boxes with slings. Tools should be lashed together with ropes or wire, and the bundles attached by ropes and slung across the saddle. Iron stakes could be carried in the same method as tools, the saddle pads we have provided would be used in each case to protect the saddles.

Method of carrying Lewis Gun Drums. It is not considered that the present method of carrying the drums can be improved, as the buckets are easily carried and provided they are correctly fastened they keep the ammunition free from dirt.

Method of carrying grenades and bombs. Every man should carry two bombs in his side pockets. These to be collected and stored at suitable points when the objective is gained.

Bombing section should carry -
Bayonet Men - Only the two bombs in side pockets.
Throwers - 6 Mills bombs in Bag slung on belt.
Remainder - 14 Mills Bombs in canvas bucket.
Rifle Grenadier Section should carry -
Every man - Wooden carriers with grenades. Cartridge carried in pocket.
Reinforcing supply of bombs. - 3 Boxes of Bombs carried on each YUKON Pack.
Reinforcing supply of rifle grenades -
(a) If No. 23 - each man would carry 2 wooden grenade carriers carrying 10 each.

continued -

5.

(b) If No 24 - Two boxes of grenades carried on each Yukon Pack.

The Signalling Officer's report on Signalling Communications is attached.

No messages received from U L H are attached.

_____ Lt. Col.
Comdg 8th Bn Royal Irish Rfles.

Certified true copy.

AJBThornton   Captain & Adjutant
8th Bn Royal Irish Rifles

1st July 1917

8th Bn. Royal Irish Rifles.

WAR DIARY

Army Form C. 2118.

July 1917.

Vol 20

Place	Date	Hour	Summary of Events and Information	Remarks and references to Appendices
Outtersteene	1-7-17		Battalion at OUTTERSTEENE. Divine Services; remainder of day holiday.	
"	2-7-17		" Day devoted to Company Training.	
"	3-7-17		" Battalion took part in a Brigade route march; distance about 8 miles. Men in excellent form.	
"	4-7-17		" Day devoted to Company Training.	
"	5-7-17		Battalion marched to CAESTRE. Distance about 7 miles; started at 7 a.m. Good day. In Billets.	
"	6-7-17		Battalion marched to RENNESCURE. Distance about 10 miles; started at 5.5 a.m. Good day; men very cheery but tired. In Billets.	
"	7-7-17		Battalion marched to LE WATTINE. Distance about 15 miles; started at 4 a.m. Good march; men very happy when they arrived.	
"	8-7-17		Battalion in camp at LE WATTINE. Morning. Divine Service. Afternoon. Platoon training. In the evening the Battalion Drums played selections in the camp; much appreciated by the men.	
"	9-7-17		" The Battalion on the range from 9 a.m. to 12 noon. on the way back. Tactical surprises were met with at both. The afternoon was devoted to Platoon Training.	

Army Form C. 2118.

8th Bn. Royal Irish Rifles. July, 1917.

WAR DIARY

~~INTELLIGENCE SUMMARY.~~

(Erase heading not required.)

Instructions regarding War Diaries and Intelligence Summaries are contained in F. S. Regs., Part II. and the Staff Manual respectively. Title pages will be prepared in manuscript.

Place	Date	Hour	Summary of Events and Information	Remarks and references to Appendices
On Service	9.7.17		The attached letter was received from G.O.C. 2nd Army and read out to the men, who were very pleased and grateful.	
"	10.7.17		The Battalion in camp at LE WATTINE. Day devoted to Company Training. The following awards were received:- 2nd Lt D.A.MOYLES. and 2nd Lt A.E.TODD – M.C. 8/12519 Rfman. (L/Cpl.) J. ARMOUR. – D.C.M. 8/13113 C.S.M. W. MOFFATT – M.C. and C.S.M. E. HILL and 8/12905. 6/10540. Sergt. J.G. McGOUGH, 17/646 Sergt L. MILLS. 17/641. Cpl. E. SAVAGE, 15/12692. Cpl. J. CUMBERLAND. 15/12556. L/Cpl. E. BORELAND, 17/490 Rfman. S. FINLAY, 8/13138 Rfman. D. McMULLAN and 8/12805 Rfman. W.J. GALWAY, the M.M.	Attached letter Rfmn J. Armour occupied the post of Bomdg & Bn. L.G. Rifles.
"	11.7.17		The Battalion in camp at LE WATTINE. Battalion trained on A.H. Area. (TILQUES AREA), moving out at 6.15 a.m.; returning to camp about 3-30 p.m.	
"	12.7.17		The Battalion in camp at LE WATTINE. Day observed as holiday. Reveille was	

WAR DIARY

8th Bn. Royal Irish Rifles.

July 1917.

Army Form C. 2118.

(Erase heading not required.)

Remarks and references to Appendices: Lt.Col. Hamilton-Lt.Col. Commdg 8th Bn. R.I. Rifles.

Place	Date	Hour	Summary of Events and Information	Remarks
Crouseilles	12-7-17		Sounded by Drums and Bugles. Sports were indulged in from 10 a.m. to 6 p.m. At 7-30 p.m. there was a Camp Concert which was attended by neighbouring Unit as well as our own Battalion. A very successful day.	
"	13-7-17		The Battalion in camp at LE WATTINE. Battalion trained on B2. TILQUES Area. Leaving at 6-15 a.m., returning about 3-45 p.m.	
"	14-7-17		at LE WATTINE. Battalion trained on A3. TILQUES Area. Leaving about 10-15 a.m., returning at 7-45 p.m.	
"	15-7-17		at LE WATTINE. Battalion on Range from 5 a.m. to 12 noon. Afternoon Divine Service. The Right Rev. Bishop Gwynne addressed the congregation during the Service.	
"	16-7-17		The Battalion in camp at LE WATTINE. Morning devoted to Company parades. Right Company night march with Enemy out; carried out on B2. TILQUES Area. March started at 10 p.m., operations finished at 1 a.m.	
"	17-7-17		Battalion withdrew to bivouac in area near ETHREM. Reveille 4 a.m. Coy. schemes, parades etc. from 5 a.m. to 10 a.m.	

8th Bn. Royal Irish Rifles.

WAR DIARY

July 1917.

Army Form C. 2118.

Instructions regarding War Diaries and Intelligence Summaries are contained in F. S. Regs., Part II. and the Staff Manual respectively. Title pages will be prepared in manuscript.

(Erase heading not required.)

Place	Date	Hour	Summary of Events and Information	Remarks and references to Appendices
On Service	17-7-17		The Battalion in camp. Battalion then marched back to camp at LA WATTINE. Battalion football team played 5th Dorset Regt (away) draw 1-1.	
"	18-7-17		" at LA WATTINE. Morning to 10.30 am. Coy parades; from that hour, day holiday for 36th Divl. Gymkhana. The Gymkhana was postponed owing to the very bad weather. In the evening, the Battalion F.T. played the 10th Corps School (away) won 1-0.	
"	19-7-17		" " LA WATTINE. Battalion trained on BL. TILQUES area, starting 12 noon, returning about 8 p.m. Battalion football team played 5th Dorset Regt. (away) return match. Won 3-0.	
"	20-7-17		The Battalion moved to QUELMES from training area. Battalion scheme was carried out. Arrived in new billets at QUELMES about 2 p.m.	
"	21-7-17		The Battalion in billets at QUELMES. Morning devoted to Company parades. Light	
"	22-7-17		Battalion took part in Brigade attack, going out about 4 p.m. returning to billets about 9 p.m., remainder of day interior economy.	

8th Bn. Royal Irish Rifles.   WAR DIARY   July 1917   Army Form C. 2118.

INTELLIGENCE SUMMARY
(Erase heading not required.)

Place	Date	Hour	Summary of Events and Information	Remarks and references to Appendices
On Service	23-7-17		The Battalion is in Billets at QUELMES. Battalion on A1. + A2. TILQUES Area from 8am to 12 noon. Coy. parades and schemes carried out. Evening Battalion fot-ball team played 12th Bn. R.I. Rifles. Whistle.	
"	24-7-17		QUELMES. Battalion took part in Brigade attack scheme. After parade the G.O.C. 36th Division presented Ribbons for the Medals to the following :- 6/10540 Sgt. J.G. McGOUGH, 17/646 Sgt. L. MILLS, 15/12692 Cpl. J. CUMBERLAND, 15/12556 L/Cpl. E. BORELAND, 17/490 Rfn. S. FINLAY, 8/13138 Rfn. D. McMULLAN and 8/12805 Rfn. W.J. GALWAY, he spoke a few nice words to each recipient, also shook hands with each one, he also addressed the 107th Brigade, speaking very highly of their very fine fighting qualities etc.	L/Cpl. Boreland 15-606 founded 8th Bn. R.I. Rifles
"	25-7-17		The Battalion moved to WINNEZEELE Area. Battalion paraded at 1-10 pm, and marched to SETQUES, at 3-30pm. Embussed and moved off to the Area, arriving there about 9-40pm. Bn. under canvas.	

8th Bn. Royal Irish Rifles.　　　WAR DIARY　　　July 1917.　　　Army Form C. 2118.

Instructions regarding War Diaries and Intelligence Summaries are contained in F. S. Regs., Part II. and the Staff Manual respectively. Title pages will be prepared in manuscript.

INTELLIGENCE SUMMARY
(Erase heading not required.)

Place	Date	Hour	Summary of Events and Information	Remarks and references to Appendices
On Service	26-7-17		Battalion in Camp in WINNEZEELE Area. Day devoted to Interior Economy. Evening, Drums and Bugle Band played selections in Camp.	
"	27-7-17		"　　"　　do.　　do.　　do.	
"	28-7-17		"　　"　　do.　　do.　　do.	
"	29-7-17		"　　"　　do.　　do.　　do.	
"	30-7-17		"　　"　Day devoted to Interior Economy. Afternoon, Drums and Bugle Band played selections in Camp. At 10 p.m. Battalion	
"	31-7-17		moved out and marched to WATOU Area, distance about 10 miles, arriving about 1.30 a.m. Weather very bad.	G.H.Hamilton Lt-Col. Comdg 8th Bn. R.I. Rifles.

A6945　Wt. W14422/M160 350,000 12/16 D. D. & L. Forms/C/2118/14.

8th Bn. Royal Irish Rifles.

WAR DIARY

August 1917   Army Form C. 2118.

Place	Date	Hour	Summary of Events and Information	Remarks and references to Appendices
On Msemreie	1.8.17		Battalion in WATOU Area. Orders to move East of YPRES were received but cancelled.	
"	2.8.17		Battalion moved by rail from POPERINGHE to West of YPRES (GOLDFISH Chateau) after detraining the Battalion marched to WIELTJE, where it occupied our Old Front Line for about two hours. At dark Battalion moved up and took over the Second Line from WEST YORKS. Not a bad relief.	
"	3.8.17		In Support. Very bad time. Heavy hostile shelling.	
"	4.8.17		do. do. do.	
"	5.8.17		do. At dark Battalion relieved the 18th Bn. Royal Irish Rifles in the Front Line.	
"	6.8.17		In the Line. Bad time. Enemy very active.	
"	7.8.17		do. Relieved at night by 9th Bn. Royal Irish Fusiliers. Bad relief. During this tour the Battalion had the following casualties:- 7 Officers and 167 O.Rks. After relief Battalion moved to a Camp at H.9.d.10.60. arriving there at about 5.30 a.m.	

Major commdg 8th Bn. Royal Irish Rifles.

8th Bn. Royal Irish Rifles.   August 1917

Army Form C. 2118.

WAR DIARY
INTELLIGENCE SUMMARY.
(Erase heading not required.)

Instructions regarding War Diaries and Intelligence Summaries are contained in F. S. Regs., Part II. and the Staff Manual respectively. Title pages will be prepared in manuscript.

Place	Date	Hour	Summary of Events and Information	Remarks and references to Appendices
Brusbrouck	8-8-'17		In Camp. Day devoted to Interior Economy.	
"	9-8-'17		do. do. do.	
"	10-8-'17		do. do. do.	
"	11-8-'17		do. Company parades and Interior Economy.	
"	12-8-'17		do. Company parades and Interior Economy and Divine Service. At night Battalion moved up to WIELTJE and took over Support Line from 9th Bn. Royal Irish Fusiliers.	
"	13-8-'17		Battalion in Support Line at WIELTJE.	
"	14-8-'17		do. do. At night Battalion withdrew to Camp at H.9.D.10.60.	
"	15-8-'17		Battalion in Camp. Day devoted to issuing stores. At night Battalion moved into Assembly Trenches at WIELTJE. Battalion in position 1 hour before zero.	
"	16-8-'17		Battalion in Assembly position. Zero hour 4-45 a.m. 108th and 109th Brigades attacked on 36th Division Front. Objectives obtained, but retired owing to opposition. Battalion on Div Support. At dark Battalion moved up and took up order from Hur 2nd Lieut Royal D. Fusiliers on frontline O'Driscoll Farm 14 R. 2nd Pls in Black line	

8th Bn. Royal Irish Rifles   August 1917.   Army Form C. 2118.

WAR DIARY

(Erase heading not required.)

Place	Date	Hour	Summary of Events and Information	Remarks and references to Appendices
On Service	17-8-17		Battalion in trenches. At night relieved by 1/5th Gloucester Regt.	Good
do.	18-8-17		relief. After relief withdrew to Camp at H.Q.D.10.60.	
do.	19-8-17		Battalion move by bus route to WINNIZEELE Area in tents.	
do.	20-8-17 to 23-8-17		Battalion in Camp at WINNIZEELE Area. do. do. do.	
do.	24-8-17		Battalion moved to BAPAUME Area by rail. Entrained at ESQUELBECQ and detrained at BAPAUME. After detraining Battalion marched to BARASTRE and encamped.	
do.	25-8-17		Battalion at BARASTRE in camp.	
do.	26-8-17		do. do. Divine Service	
do.	27-8-17		Battalion moved to camp at YTRES.	
do.	28-8-17		Battalion moved into Divisional Reserve at EQUANCOURT. Amalgamation with 9th Bn. Royal Irish Rifles took place on arrival at EQUANCOURT.	
do.	29-8-17 to 31-8-17		Battalion in camp at EQUANCOURT. Company parades and reorganisation. do. do.	

www.ingramcontent.com/pod-product-compliance
Lightning Source LLC
Chambersburg PA
CBHW081546160426
43191CB00011B/1853